THE LOV

C000262858

La

THE ART OF BETTER LOVEMAKING

THE LOVERS' GUIDE

Laid Bare

THE ART OF BETTER LOVEMAKING

Completely revised and updated
Second Edition published 2011 by Lifetime Books
in association with Bookshaker (Cabal Group Limited)
Lifetime Productions International Ltd
CPC1, Capital Park,
Fulbourn, Cambridge
CB21 5XE UK

First published in Great Britain in 1992 by Sidgwick and
Jackson Ltd a division of Pan MacMillan Publishers Ltd

Editor: Robert Page
Consultant: Dr Andrew Stanway
Illustrator: Christopher O Page

British Library Cataloguing in Publication Data
3 5 7 9 10 8 6 4

A catalogue record of this book is available
from the British Library
978 1 907498 66 4

www.loversguide.com

CONTENTS

THREE: MAKING LOVE

FOUR: THE OTHER SIDE OF SEX

FIVE: KEEPING SEX ALIVE

FOREWORD

Sex interests us all. Yet for most of us, our personal sex lives are often regarded as private - something to be kept behind closed doors and rarely discussed. For this reason, it can be difficult to learn what we want to know about sex in an open, helpful and constructive way.

When the producers at Lifetime asked me to host the first of *The Lovers' Guide* programs, we set out to create a modern series that would try, sensitively and authoritatively, to bring sex into the open. The advent of video made it possible to bring intimate pictures into the privacy of our own homes, so that now everyone can improve, or confirm, their personal knowledge of practical sexuality.

The Lovers' Guide is now distributed all over the world. Predictably, such an explicit and honest visual representation of sex has caused a stir, but millions of people have now seen the videos, and the feedback has been hugely positive.

"Thank you for giving me permission to do things we'd been doing for years, but felt guilty and anxious about..."

"Thank you for helping us feel better about ourselves by making us realise that what we wanted - but hadn't dared - to do is normal."

"Please keep up the good work; it really got us talking like nothing else."

These are only some of the kinds of comments I get as I travelled the world, listening to what people thought and felt about *The Lovers' Guide* videos.

Video, though, is but one medium of communication. This is why *The Lovers' Guide* has been made into a book for those who may want to approach the messages more thoroughly than the spoken word allows, and then perhaps to turn to the videos for reference.

The Lovers' Guide book takes the same simple and straightforward approach to practical sex, preferred by most people. It is honest, authoritative and pulls no punches. With greater knowledge and understanding of sexuality, with openness, trust and better communication between one another, every couple can build a more successful and lasting one-to-one relationship.

I hope this book will help as many people as the videos have, and empower individuals everywhere to reach greater fulfillment in their sexual lives.

Dr Andrew Stanway
Consultant to *The Lovers' Guide*

INTRODUCTION

This fully updated, all new, second edition of the original bestselling *Lovers' Guide* book marks the twentieth anniversary of the brand that has helped enhance millions of people's love lives. Indeed *The Lovers' Guide* is not only still going strong, but remains at the forefront of technology with the latest film being made in 3-D and this volume being released as an e-book.

The Lovers' Guide story began in 1991 when the then Director of the British Board of Film Classification, James Ferman, made the unprecedented decision to support making the first of these ground-breaking films. He immediately understood our ethic – an educational, authoritative yet sensual product for all men and women who wanted to understand more about sex and relationships. With Dr Andrew Stanway, a distinguished expert in this field, and the (then) Family Planning Association consulting on the script, our credentials for the granting of an 18 certificate were assured, and filming began on what was then the most open and frank film of its kind ever.

When that original *Lovers' Guide* – the first educational film to show explicit adult sexual activity – was allowed to go on public sale on the high street, the impact was huge. It became the best selling non-fiction title in the UK on VHS ever, selling over a million copies, with a copy in almost one in six homes in the UK. It has since gone into 22 other countries and been translated into 13 languages: there have been 12 subsequent films, three books, including an encyclopedia, TV documentaries, and the biggest website in the world dedicated to sex and relationships - *www.loversguide.com*.

At the start, outraged by its success, many were quick to go on the attack. They claimed that *The Lovers' Guide* was really porn dressed as adult education. Certainly, *The Lovers' Guide* is erotic to some extent – where would sex be if the sight of naked bodies didn't get pulses racing? But its purpose is completely different to pornography. The goal of *The Lovers' Guide* is to explain, not excite. It is not there for the simple purpose of aiding arousal, but to show two equal individuals how to make the best, and most caring, love of their lives. Indeed, it was because of this approach, intended to develop people's sexual repertoire and enhance their relationships, that *The Lovers' Guide* was mostly taken up by women, who accounted for up to 75% of sales.

Equally because of its success, many others were quick to copy us. Imitation may be the sincerest form of flattery, and in the twenty years since we exploded onto the scene there have been a vast number of look-alikes, though most have fallen by the wayside while *The Lovers' Guide* has remained. Of course the internet has vastly increased access to any amount of sexual material, yet while online porn allows us to see just about any possible coupling imaginable, it doesn't provide any of the guidance and authoritative insights offered by *The Lovers' Guide* about how to improve one's own lovemaking, and get more, real life, pleasure.

In this book, we have tried to distill the essence of *The Lovers' Guide* approach. We encourage readers to explore their sexuality, engage in new techniques and expand their horizons. In doing so they can keep their repertoire continually revitalised, their sex lives refreshed and their relationships deeply fulfilled. Good sex may not be the only key to a happy love life – but it certainly helps. And *The Lovers' Guide* mission is to allow everyone to experience the best sex of their lives. Enjoy!

Robert Page
Creator and Producer *The Lovers' Guide*

ONE
UNDERSTANDING EACH OTHER

How our sexuality develops. You can get the most out of your relationship by appreciating one another's physical and emotional needs and understanding male and female differences. This helps to overcome shyness and inhibition and helps you both relax.

We are all sexual creatures. Sex is a natural activity to be enjoyed and need not involve guilt, fear or danger.

THE SEXUAL SELF

Every person's sexual psyche is determined and influenced by a unique combination of biological and psychological factors. Development begins before birth and continues throughout life, although gender role models in early stages are important influences. Men and women are not the same psychologically; whilst there are basic similarities, there are also fundamental differences.

Female biology and evolution

Each month a woman produces one ovum in contrast to a man's almost infinite supply of sperm; and women tend to lose their fertility (although not their sex drive) earlier in life. As well as this, they may be aware, often unconsciously, of their reproductive role. This can have an effect on a woman's attitude to her partner. On a practical level, modern contraception means that sex doesn't have to lead to offspring, but this deep-seated instinct may account for women being, statistically, less likely to engage in casual sex than men, and more likely to look for a committed relationship. This sense of commitment may include a greater need for non-sexual signs of affection and emotional involvement.

Female attitudes to sex

Our ideas of men and women's roles are often influenced by the idea that vaginal intercourse is the most important sexual act. This may cause problems for women as well as men. If a man feels under pressure to perform, he may feel he needs to take a dominant role while the woman remains passive. For some couples, or at some times, this may be ideal for both, but many women want to be more active or dominant, at least some of the time, just as many men may like to take a less active role. This can also make men uncomfortable expressing the tenderness and affection which his partner may need to feel. Some women feel under pressure to climax in sex which can lead to a "faked" orgasm.

Female arousal

Sexual arousal for a woman tends to be more complex than for a man. A woman's whole body can be an erogenous zone, with areas of particular sensitivity varying from one woman to another. Visual stimuli are important but in a different way than for men, as women tend to respond more to atmosphere and situations. Research suggests that women can reach a higher state of arousal from fantasy than men.

For a long time, ideas of femininity have been centred around a woman's appearance as the source of her attractiveness. Consequently, a woman's self-image is often influenced by how she feels about her looks and, in particular, her figure. Changing perceptions of women's place in society, though, have given greater value to a woman's sense of personal achievement.

Male biology and evolution

Men's attitude to sexual partners may be affected by their almost infinite supply of sperm, as opposed to a woman having only one ovum to fertilize each month. This is thought to be what makes men tend to be less bound by emotional commitment until they finally decide to settle down. Until this point a man may feel no biological need of commitment and this may explain why, statistically, men are more likely to have casual sex and be able to enjoy sex without commitment. Studies have shown that men tend to fall in and out of love more quickly and easily than women.

Male attitudes to sex

Because it has been necessary for reproduction, we put great emphasis on vaginal sexual intercourse as the most important sexual act. This can put great pressure on the heterosexual man. He feels that he has to achieve and maintain an erection and 'perform' in a dominant manner. He may feel under pressure to make sure his partner reaches orgasm every time. Many men are also concerned about the size of their penis.

The 'ideal' image of sex, with its stress on vaginal intercourse and male performance, is both unrealistic and, in many cases, undesirable, as it excludes many more exciting and sensuous – as well as the often more satisfying – aspects of sex play. It also ignores same gender sex.

Male arousal

Male sexual arousal is – relatively speaking – direct and immediate. Men's erogenous zones are specific and men tend to respond to specific triggers. Both stimulation and arousal are focused more on the genitals. Visual stimuli also tend to be more important for men than they are for women, which may be why pornographic magazines and films tend to be more popular with, and oriented toward, men. Men tend to have stronger voyeuristic tendencies for the same reason.

Notions of masculinity

Each man has his own idea of what it means to be masculine, influenced both by his cultural influences and by gender role models. The 'macho' man has long been a powerful image, but men are also expected to be more sensitive, openly caring and not afraid to express their emotions. Men can find keeping the balance between these two aspects of behaviour confusing, and in particular how they should behave toward a sexual partner of either gender.

SEXUAL ORIENTATION

The terms 'heterosexual', 'homosexual' and 'bisexual' are commonly used to classify people in terms of their sexual orientation. However, the terms really refer not to people but to types of behaviour, and their use to classify people has lead to countless cases of misunderstanding and misrepresentation. Sexual orientation is not a simple matter: human sexuality cannot be divided into distinct groups. Understanding these terms and what they really mean can help people to express their own sexuality more completely as well as to understand that of others.

Describing sexuality

Homosexuality refers to sexual attraction to, or relations with, a member or members of the same sex; heterosexuality is with the opposite sex; bisexuality is with members of both sexes. Any of these behaviours can encompass everything from the occasional fantasy to full sexual relations.

The American sex researcher, Dr Alfred Kinsey, devised a seven-point scale from 0 to 6 to describe human sexual orientation more precisely: 0 represented people who were exclusively heterosexual; 6 represented those who were exclusively homosexual; and 3 applied to those who were equally attracted to men and women. Ratings 1, 2, 4 and 5 deal with all other degrees of preference, and take into account such factors as fantasies and isolated or one-off experiences outside a person's usual sexual preference. The system also deals with changes in preference throughout life. Many people are curious about other kinds of sexual experience and experiment at some time with different kinds of sexual activity. Ultimately, those who rate themselves at 0 or 6 are relatively few.

Which way?

It is increasingly believed that few, if any, people are exclusively homosexual or heterosexual. Human sexuality does not work within tight definitions or limitations – it can take many different forms and is fluid and flexible.

Kinsey's studies produced statistics suggesting that about 37% of males and 13% of females had some overt homosexual experience in the course of adult life, although his methods of gathering information have since been called into question. It is estimated that exclusively homosexual males comprise about 5% of the adult population. The proportion of homosexual women is likely to be marginally less than this. A recent study in the UK indicated that 92.3% of men and 95.1% of women describe their sexual experience as 'only heterosexual'. It is also known that homo-erotic fantasy is common among people of all sexual orientations.

What determines sexual orientation?

There is a great deal of prejudice about sexual orientation. In most cultures such prejudice is a relatively recent phenomenon, as different kinds of attraction have always been part of human sexuality. There are a number of factors which suggest that non-heterosexual sexualities are a natural consequence of biology and/or psychology.

Records of homosexual activity have been found in all periods and a great many cultural groups. Even where it was not socially acceptable, it seems that it still occurred and the proportions of different types of sexuality seem to be approximately the same in all cultural and racial groups. Homosexual activity has been observed among other higher primates, including at times when opportunities for heterosexual activity were readily available.

Various research studies point to a genetic basis for sexuality. Studies of identical and non-identical twins (identical twins have identical genetic makeup) show that if one twin is homosexual, an identical brother is much more likely to be homosexual than a non-identical brother. More recent research claims to have identified the relevant gene.

Male homosexuality has also been linked to the amount of testosterone available in the womb. There are also possible links to the number of male siblings; a study has shown that the greater the number of older brothers that a man has, the more likely he is to be homosexual. The reasons could either be biological or simply an effect within the family.

A lack of admiration for, or a lack of desire to be like, the same-sex parent has been linked to homosexual tendencies. And puritanical attitudes towards sex, if they lead to a deeply rooted fear of the opposite sex, may also encourage homosexual behaviour.

The term 'homosexual' strictly applies to any kind of sexual behaviour – from fantasy to intercourse – with a member of the same sex, but it may be used to refer to a person who is exclusively or primarily attracted to or involved with same-sex partners. In many cultures there are strong taboos relating to all forms of homosexuality; these are largely due to misunderstandings and misconceptions.

The term 'gay' is frequently used to describe homosexuals, particularly men. The term 'lesbian' is used for homosexual women.

It is not possible to identify a person as gay or lesbian by appearance. Though some gay men and women play up 'camp' or 'butch' roles, many do not. There are no specific gay or lesbian 'types'; people who enjoy homosexual activity are as varied in terms of occupation, social class, dress, religion and education as anyone else.

Gays and lesbians are no more likely to carry out sexual crimes than anyone else, indeed, homosexual men are statistically less likely to abuse children than heterosexuals.

Homosexual relationships are as varied as heterosexual relationships in terms of affection, physicality and commitment. Similarly, gay sex is just as, if not more, varied than heterosexual sex. Practices include kissing, touching, body-rubbing, oral sex, masturbation and – between men – anal intercourse.

Even in Western society there are few places where people can be open about homosexuality, although acceptance tends to be greater where there are fewer religious restraints and in large, more cosmopolitan cities. In some societies homosexuality is illegal.

As a result, in many larger towns and cities gay and lesbian meeting places have been created. As for heterosexuals, some are for general socializing while others are intended specifically for finding partners, sometimes for casual sex. These venues include bars, restaurants, and some parks, steam baths and specific public toilets.

Transvestism

Transvestites are men and women who like to dress in the clothes associated with the opposite gender, either occasionally or, in a few cases, all the time. Most transvestites are male and heterosexual; many are married with children.

In many cases, cross-dressing is a form of fetishism, with a sexual attachment to the clothing and accessories of the opposite sex, which in themselves may produce strong sexual arousal.

Other cases have to do with a man wishing to express the feminine side of his personality; women's clothing provides a sense of freedom and security, together with a release from the demands of the male gender role. This seems to be particularly common among homosexual transvestites. It may also be a way of challenging traditional gender roles, which determine many forms of dress and other aspects of behaviour.

Cross-dressing may be practised in public or in private, with or without the knowledge of a sexual partner. It is believed that it is usually carried out in secret and to be not uncommon.

Transsexualism or gender dysphoria

Transsexualism is a rare condition. Being transsexual means having an overwhelming sense of having been born with the body of the wrong sex. Transsexuals may cross-dress, but their attitude to their body and in particular their genitals is completely different from that of a transvestite. Transsexuals usually wish to disassociate themselves from their bodies, even to the point of having their physical sex reassigned by means of surgery.

Transsexuals often tend to be very conservative with regard to perceptions of gender roles, seeing male and female roles as quite distinct. They are likely to see themselves as heterosexual, being attracted to members of the opposite sex in terms of their sexual identity even though this is the same biological sex, although there are bisexual and homosexual transsexuals.

Once a person is convinced that he or she is transsexual, there are various courses of action open to them. For most, the ultimate goal is to have surgery to bring their body into line with their sexual identify: this is known as a sex change or gender reassignment.

LEARNING ABOUT SEX

Childhood

We get much of our early sexual information (right or wrong) from our peers. While girls usually learn to masturbate on their own, many boys learn with their peers. By adolescence, nine out of ten boys are masturbating, though this tends to be less common among girls. Many boys and girls are curious about the genitals of the opposite sex, although penises seem to attract more attention among both sexes.

Mutual kissing and fondling are common, as are pelvic thrusting, simulated intercourse and mutual masturbation. Intercourse is more rare, but has been known to occur. Activity may be heterosexual or homosexual, but the choice of partner or orientation is unlikely to be significant at this stage. It may be spontaneous or it may be imitative, influenced by sexual activity seen on television or intimacy between parents or other adults. Surveys suggest that as many as 85% of adults recall some sort of sex play with peers between the ages of six and twelve. Personal, romantic attachments before the age of six are not uncommon.

Attitudes to childhood sexuality

In many cultures, childhood sexuality is either ignored or repressed. There are relatively few in which it is openly accepted as natural and healthy, although tolerance does seem to be increasing. Many societies have progressed from times when children were often forcibly restrained or punished for innocent masturbation. In a very few cultural groups, sexual activity is actively encouraged from an early age.

The attitudes of parents and other carers to children's sexuality can be very powerful. Children learn from them how they ought to behave and, if they are taught that sexual feelings are dirty or shameful, this impression often remains with them for life. A parent or carer who is comfortable with his or her own body and sexuality will pass on this message to the child, who will learn that sex is natural and to be enjoyed without guilt or shame at an appropriate time.

Sexuality in Adolescence

Adolescence begins with puberty, when the adult hormonal cycles are set in motion, bringing with them the range of physical and psychological changes that herald the development from child to young adult. The physical changes are the most immediately noticeable, but they bring with them the need for psychological and social adjustment. It is often a time of intense confusion but it can also be exciting. Puberty usually lasts between three and five years, from the ages of nine to thirteen in girls and ten to fifteen in boys. Some studies have suggested that the age at which puberty occurs is gradually getting lower worldwide. Puberty sees the development of the secondary sexual characteristics differentiating male and female, and is marked by the menarche or first menstruation in girls and the first ejaculation (spermarche) in boys.

It is usually at puberty that young people start to become sexually aware and/or active. Watersheds such as girl's first menstruation or a boy's first ejaculation can be exciting or traumatic, depending on the kind of attitudes and information which the girl or boy has experienced. The development of other physical characteristics also has its impact. Physical awareness increases, as does a sense of personal and sexual attractiveness, which may acquire a disproportionate amount of importance at this time. Adolescents who do not consider themselves attractive may find it harder to relate to their peers.

Social and psychological changes

Adolescence includes the development of identity, both personal and sexual. It is a time for developing personal, social and sexual-confidence and learning to relate to prospective partners.

Adolescence also signifies a shift away from the family's emotional support and personal influence in favour of peer groups and other, non-familial, role models. An enormous variety of influences are experienced, and young adults have to choose between them as they forge their own identity and attitudes. This is part of becoming more individual and independent.

At the same time, sexual identity, attitudes and values are forming. Adolescence is often a time of experimentation as people try out different gender and sexual roles until they find one with which they are comfortable. It is often a time for experimenting with different kinds of sexual orientation; transsexuals may also become acutely aware of their condition at this stage. This search for identity may continue until much later in life. Social pressures may prevent a person from exploring their identity and sexuality, particularly at this delicate stage of development and, above all, if the kinds of identity in question are perceived as outside the norm of the wider cultural group.

COMMUNICATING ABOUT SEX

When I first moved in with Mike, it seemed like we just lived for sex. But after a few months, I began to worry that I wasn't feeling satisfied, though I couldn't bring myself to talk to him about it, in case he got upset or angry with me. Then one night, when I wasn't feeling at all sexy when he wanted to make love, I just blurted it out. I told him I wanted him to touch me, and arouse me first. He put his arms round me and told me that he loved me. He knew something had been wrong, but didn't know what it was. I was so relieved. Since then, we've talked about what we both wanted from sex - we even wrote a list of things to do, and our sex life has improved enormously.

Rosie

Most people's greatest sexual problem is that they find it difficult to communicate to their partner exactly what they feel, or want.

For a relationship to be truly fulfilling for both partners, there must be mutual understanding.

Countless surveys show that communication problems rank highest on the list of reasons people give for lack of satisfaction in their relationships. Talking about sex, however, is not easy - especially when it involves our very own sexuality rather than sex in general. Sex is mostly so private that, even in intimate relationships, couples can feel awkward about revealing their sexual needs, desires and anxieties. But if they can break down these barriers, they invariably find that the emotional side of their life together grows stronger, and their lovemaking becomes much better.

Listen first, talk second

Communication between two people has more to do with listening than talking. And listening constructively can be very difficult, especially when the subject is a delicate one, such as sex and relationships. Although this can affect both men and women, on average more women complain that they are often misunderstood by their partners.

The first thing we must do is to put our ego to one side; too often, our own opinions can get in the way and prevent us from really hearing what our partner is trying to say.

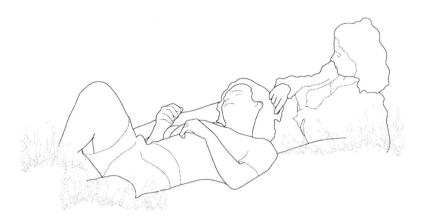

Try to set aside time to talk about, and listen to one another. If it helps, choose a neutral location such as a quiet dinner out or a walk in the country.

Make the time

The earlier you start communicating in your relationship, the better for you both. All too often, something that has been bottled up by one partner suddenly gets thrown into an argument about a completely different subject. As a result, one of you can be so badly hurt that the subject becomes a no-go area for any further mention, let alone proper discussion.

It is always worth investing time in talking, and more importantly, *listening*, to one another in a loving relationship Try to set aside special times, such as date nights together when you can both feel at ease to discuss your emotions and feelings. Agree on a location where you will both feel comfortable – on neutral territory, whether out of the house, such as a walk in the country, a quiet dinner out, or at home with all communication devices switched off.

Take things slowly. You won't be able to deal with every issue in one go - and if a certain subject should become difficult for one or both of you, save it for later and move on to another. You can always come back to it when you have had more time to sort out your thoughts and work through your feelings and attitudes. You could be surprised how much you agree, although you had never dared to express your true feelings before.

Listen to your partner; put yourself in their shoes and reflect back what you hear and observe. Along with this, try to become aware of the non-verbal communication that is your partner's body language. Your verbal and non-verbal feedback can be very helpful, and he or she can feel much better understood. You could be pleased and surprised by how well you start to communicate with one another, even on very difficult subjects.

OVERCOMING INHIBITIONS

At first I was really shocked when Annie told me what she wanted from me when it came to sex. Until then, I'd just assumed that what was great for me went for her too. I guess we just hadn't talked properly about sex, and there were things that I liked which she didn't. Once we found out where we both stood - what, I suppose, our hang-ups were - it was surprising how much it helped with overcoming them. And now, one hang-up we don't have is not being able to talk about our sex life.

James

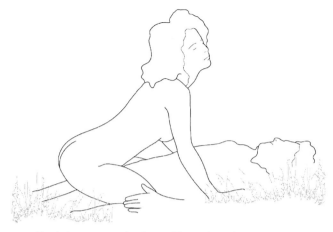

Many men like their partner to take charge of lovemaking, for example by being on top. Some women, however, can be inhibited about taking control like this, thinking it makes them appear pushy or too highly sexed; expressing and discussing these worries can help them to overcome such inhibitions.

Oral sex is considered by many people to be the most intimate form of love play. Often, it is only within a truly trusting relationship that the full pleasures can be realised.

Overcoming inhibitions about some aspect of your sex life –
whether engaging in oral sex, trying different lovemaking
positions, or something as simple as making love with the
lights on – often begins only with sharing your concerns with
a loving partner you trust intimately. It is essential to work
through any problems together. Don't even think of trying to
cajole a partner into trying something; - blackmail of the 'If
you really loved me you would…' variety puts a severe strain
on any relationship and never works.

SENSUAL MASSAGE

*I don't always feel at my best after a tiring day at work and often
the last thing on my mind is sex. I'm too wound up for anything,
really. But somehow Rob can always get me relaxed with a
massage. When he's working my muscles, I can honestly say that
all my tension gets released and I feel alive and sexy again. I end
up enjoying every moment he's stroking me - he's very good, you
know. He never pushes me into having sex with him, although
after a massage I am more likely to want to make love. Massage
for both of us is an important way of getting closer and staying
close.*

Charlotte

One of the best ways to discover one another's bodies is through
massage. It is a satisfying form of loving behaviour in itself, and
can be a sensuous prelude to lovemaking. In simple terms,
massage is a structured way of touching each other, a beautiful
way to get closer and a good way of learning to surrender.

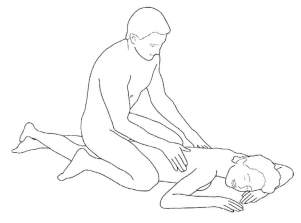

(1) Begin by lightly but firmly massaging your partner's back, keeping both hands in contact with the body on either side of the spine. Use oils or talcum powder to help your hands slide more smoothly and always keep up a steady, soothing rhythm. Straddling your partner while you do this means he or she can feel the pleasurable warmth from your inner thighs.

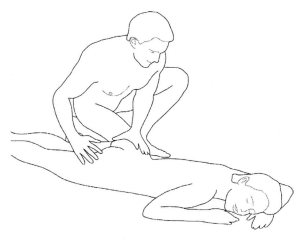

(2) Next, move down to your partner's buttocks where you can knead the fleshy parts quite firmly. The inside of the thighs is a highly erogenous area, so spend some time softly stroking here as your partner becomes even more relaxed. When you have worked all over your partner's body, start again, using a different technique.

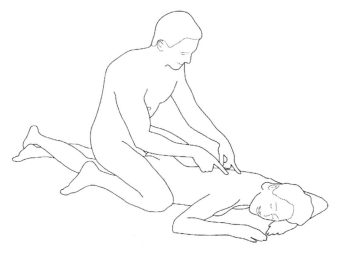

(3) Using your fingers lightly to give feathery touches down the back can add quite different erotic sensations. Experiment with different touches and discover what your partner likes best.

The aim is to produce relaxing and pleasurable sensations for the partner receiving, although naturally the giver also benefits, so spend time softly stroking for the other person's pleasure and the joy of giving.

Choose a place that is warm and comfortable, and a time when you will not be disturbed. Don't worry too much about technique, but learn from each other what feels best. Do not massage bony areas - stick to the fleshy parts and try to be firm but gentle. Listen to your partner's sounds of pleasure to guide you. Use soothing oils, or talcum powder, to make your hands slide smoothly over your partner's body, and try to maintain a steady, connected and flowing rhythm.

Sensual massage, done with love and care, builds trust in a way almost nothing else can. You become used to seeing your partner totally naked; you learn to trust him or her to handle you with reverence and respect; you learn to relax in someone else's company; and you can give and receive love and bodily pleasure without any pressure to have sexual intercourse.

Taking it further

If the mood is right, and one or other of you wants to take things further, it can be fun to make sensual massage more erotic. You could try using a feather, fur or even some melting ice. Run your hair, your breasts, your penis, over your partner's body. Again, always be guided by the receiver. Approach everything with your mind open, and your body relaxed, and you may be surprised to find out just which parts of your body give you the most sensual feelings.

With practice and imagination, your instincts will take you into new and exciting realms of pleasure.

I go through phases. First I feel relaxed and rather dreamy as I let myself go completely, and then I start to feel really turned on. I'm almost desperate for Natalie to grab hold of my penis, but she just tantalisingly ignores it as she keeps massaging my front. It really is very erotic and I just can't wait to make love to her.

Simon

(1) Try not to ignore any part of your lover's body. Massaging feet and toes, hands and fingers, is wonderfully relaxing, and can often create exceptional erotic feelings.

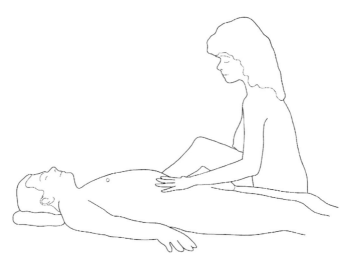

(2) When your partner is on his or her back, work along the chest, and thighs - but make sure that you ignore the genitals. And do not forget the neck and face; use firm but gentle touches here. After massaging his or her entire body with your hands, use other parts of your body to give your lover different sensations.

(3) The woman drawing her breasts and nipples gently across her lover's body can provide exquisitely sexy sensations. The man's penis on his partner can have similar effects.

EXPLORING EACH OTHER

Before Marie, I guess I'd always been a bit wary of oral sex with other girls. Then one night, just as we were about to get on with our usual sex, I moved down between her legs and started kissing her there. I guess I just wanted to know her fully. She told me where she liked being touched the most, and for the first time I started to lick and touch her in a way I hadn't done before. Now I've learned what she really likes, this has added so much to our sex life for both of us.

Steve

Having learned how to appreciate one another naked, it is very helpful to get to know the way around each other's genitals and patterns of arousal.

This should happen fairly naturally at an early stage of a committed sexual relationship, but if years have gone by without it, it's never too late. Mutual exploration at any time can bring real insights and benefits.

One day, as part of foreplay, when you are feeling really relaxed, try to overcome any shyness or inhibitions, and take turns to explore one another's genitals in some detail. Have a bath or shower, so you are fresh and clean. Take your time, keep the room warm, and make yourselves comfortable, on the bed or sofa. Be sure you won't be interrupted by visitors or the phone.

The Vulva and Clitoris

The man should begin by simply looking at the outside of his partner's genitals - the vulva and the clitoris. He will first see the outer lips, or labia majora, which can be opened with your fingers to reveal the smaller ones, or labia minora, inside. These come together at the top to form a little hood which covers the tip of the clitoris. This is a highly sensitive organ; for most women, clitoral stimulation is the best, and sometimes the only, way to achieve orgasm.

A man can begin getting to know his partner's genitals by
looking at her vulva and clitoris as a normal part of foreplay.

What looks like an indentation, or even a small hole beneath
the head of the clitoris is the opening to the urinary passage,
or urethra. Below this is the more obvious and larger hole
which is the entrance to the vagina, and still further back, lies
the stretch of skin, or perineum, which leads to the anus,
Around the opening of the vagina there are sometimes small
flaps of skin not to be confused with the labia. These are the
remains of the hymen - the membrane that sealed off the
vaginal opening before your partner first had sex, or first used
a tampon. In many women they may be very small and all
but invisible to the untrained eye.

After looking comes feeling.

Go back up to her clitoris, and run your finger lightly over the body of the organ just above its head. It will probably feel like the small rubber end of a pencil. Now lovingly touch the inner and outer lips and see what they feel like. Run your fingers along the two pairs of lips and then around the vaginal opening. Stroke the perineum – the bridge of tissue between the vagina and anus.

(1) Run your fingers up towards the clitoris to see how it is enclosed in its small hood, just beneath the head of the clitoris is the entrance to the urinary tract. Now softly squeeze the outer lips between your fingers, to discover how they feel.

(2) Gently insert a finger into the vagina and feel its walls and then insert it further until you can feel the cervix – the neck of the womb. Try a 'come hither' motion to massage the front wall of the vagina and try to locate a slightly swollen area of tissue that is the woman's G-spot.

UNDERSTANDING EACH OTHER

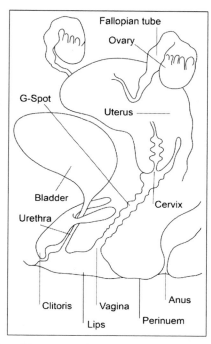

The anatomy of a woman's sexual organs

The Vagina

Gently insert a finger into the vagina and feel its walls; they will be wet and slightly ridged, especially along the front wall, up towards the woman's stomach. When a woman is unaroused, the walls of the vagina lie flat against each other and are usually around four inches deep. When she becomes aroused the walls lubricate and move apart, and the space in the vagina increases.

The Woman's G-Spot

On the front wall of the vagina there may be a sensitive area called the G-Spot, which gives pleasure when stroked. It is best stimulated by a come-hither motion of the index finger and, if excited for long enough, can help bring some women to orgasm. To begin with, though, you may not be able to feel it unless the woman is aroused, as it swells up to form a distinct area only after lots of stimulation. Caressing the G-Spot can trigger a sensation like wanting to pass water; this may come as a surprise the first time, but she is likely to learn to distinguish the two different sensations.

The G Spot's existence remains controversial and some think that it is really part of the clitoris, a much bigger organ than previously realised, that can be stimulated from the inside.

Now gently push your finger in a little more, until you come to something that feels like the tip of your nose. This is the cervix, or neck of the womb; and you might also find that you feel it with the head of your penis during intercourse when you penetrate very deeply.

The Penis

A man's genitals are mostly more external and so much easier to see. Again, and as a normal part of foreplay, it is useful to take the trouble to explore them in detail The woman should start by looking at the penis itself, as the most obvious part. Begin by looking at it when it is not erect, and watch it change as an erection grows. Then gently pull back the foreskin – if there is one (if there isn't, and the head is fully exposed even when the penis is in its flaccid state, the man has been circumcised) - to reveal the glans or head. At its tip is the opening that lets out both urine and semen, the urethra, and just underneath this is a little vertical ridge of skin, the frenum. Most men say that this is their most arousing part, because it is packed with nerve endings.

(1) Begin by looking at the penis when it is limp.

(2) Then watch how it changes as it erects. Take notice of how the
muscles of the scrotum - the bag of skin holding the testicles -
tighten under the skin and the testicles move about.

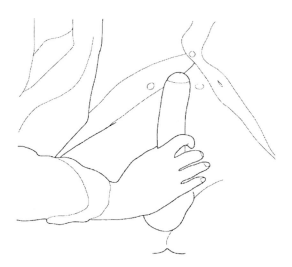

(3) If the man has a foreskin, pull it back to reveal the glans.
At the lip is a small hole that lets out both urine and semen, the urethra.

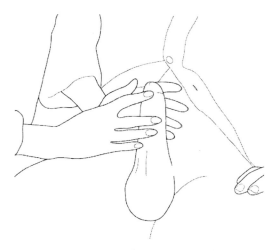

(4) Run your thumb or finger around the ridge of the glans and touch the
vertical ridge of skin that runs from the shaft to the glans - the frenum.
For many men this is the most sensitive part of the penis.

UNDERSTANDING EACH OTHER

(5) Feel around the base of the penis to find the 'root' that runs back towards the anus and around the anal area, the perineum.

At first I felt a bit shy with Paul, and didn't know what to do with his penis. But one time, I reached down and gently squeezed his balls. He didn't have to tell me how much he really liked me doing this! Since then I've discovered more and more of what he likes, and sex has become much more fun.

Ellie

The Testicles

Next, turn your attention to the bag of skin, or scrotum, that contains his balls, or testicles. You might be able to see the muscles in the scrotum contract under the skin, and the testicles move about.

Now gently feel those: they are largely a mass of coiled tubes, containing sperm that are maturing in readiness for ejaculation. At the top of each ball is a

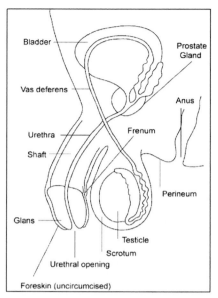

The anatomy of a man's sexual organs

hard core which you can feel between your finger and thumb. This is the vas deferens - the tube which conveys sperm to the glans of the penis at the moment of ejaculation. Now move to the base of the penis and feel all around it. You will notice that the penis has a sort of root that goes back towards the anus. Run your fingers along this, the perineum, and around the anal area.

The Man's G-Spot

The man has a G-Spot, too, but given that it is located on the front wall of the inside of the lower bowel in his anus, you may both want to think how far you wish to go in trying to locate it. Should you wish to go ahead, you can reach it with a well lubricated finger, and the man relaxing his anal

UNDERSTANDING EACH OTHER

opening or sphincter. You will feel his prostate gland as a firm lump of tissue, about the size of a walnut, situated in the front wall of the rectum, or back passage. Gentle stimulation with the pad of the finger can create exquisite sensations and intense orgasms for a man. Some even say that it alters the whole orgasmic experience for them.

...AND AFTERWARDS

Make these exploration sessions part of your foreplay and arousal; take time and, if you're both happy with it, share what you have discovered. Being this open with one another shows real affection, acceptance and interest in each other, and such intimate knowledge can draw you very much closer.

AROUSAL AND ORGASM

I won't forget the time I first had sex with Sharon. There was real electricity between us - we'd been flirting all evening, and then suddenly she took me by surprise and kissed me on the neck in a way that sent a shiver right through me. I thought I wouldn't be able to hold back a second longer. I was actually holding her close to me, and I could feel her nipples getting hard as I started stroking her breasts. And then slowly she started to pull off my shirt and push down my pants and trousers to reveal my throbbing erection. By now I was bursting, but I managed to undress her slowly, in the same way, By the time we made love, we were both so turned on - it was the best orgasm I'd ever bad.

Mark

Some time spent on foreplay is essential for both partners to be fully aroused. Whilst the man can usually respond with an erection very quickly, the woman usually needs some time before her vagina is fully lubricated and ready to accept his penis. Orgasms are also more likely for the woman if she is fully aroused before penetration and, with more time spent on foreplay, the man can benefit from bigger, firmer erections.

The first big step on the journey through our sexual life is to accept our own body, care for it and respect it. This helps our sense of self-esteem and is a compliment to our partner. It shows that, by caring about and for ourselves, we care about them. A caring and sincere partner will always be more satisfying than one who just looks sexy.

Accepting ourselves also means acknowledging that we all have sexual needs; understanding our own, and our partner's, is important in building long-term, intimate, relationships.

Our first major encounter with our sexuality is usually during masturbation, an activity in which almost everyone indulges, if only from time to time. Masturbation can provide not only beneficial physical relief, ensuring that everything is in working order, but it is also an important milestone to help us understand the changes that occur in our bodies when we feel sexually aroused and move toward orgasm.

Human sexual response can be divided into five phases: *resting, excitement, plateau, orgasm* and *resolution*. During foreplay, excitement increases in both men and women until they reach the plateau phase. Women generally take longer than men to reach this phase, which is why extended foreplay is so important. From the plateau phase, both men and women move towards orgasm.

After orgasm, the man's resolution phase is short, perhaps only two or three minutes, until he returns to the unaroused resting phase. For the woman, resolution is slow and gradual, often lasting up to half an hour. Some women can delay this phase, and return to the plateau phase where they can be stimulated again to have another, multiple, orgasm.

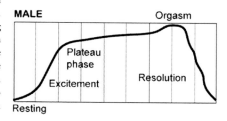

MALE

Orgasm

Plateau phase

Excitement

Resolution

Resting

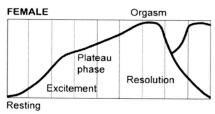

FEMALE

Orgasm

Plateau phase

Excitement

Resolution

Resting

Man's Arousal

For a man, visual stimuli are a highly effective trigger for sexual arousal: bare skin, revealing clothes, even red lipstick, can do the trick. But we should not forget the power of the other senses. The sense of smell is more powerful than many think, though hearing words of passion can also be very arousing, as can touching one another's, and our own, erogenous zones.

The first obvious sign of a man's arousal is an erection: blood fills the tissue in the penis, causing it to stiffen and grow longer and thicker. As arousal increases so does the heart rate, breathing quickens and the nostrils flare.

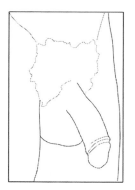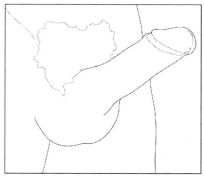

Words, sounds, smell and particularly sight can all trigger a man's erection. As he becomes aroused, blood flows into his penis and is trapped, causing it to grow thicker and longer. In its erect state, the penis naturally points upwards.

Other changes may occur in a man's body during sexual activity. About a quarter of men develop a sex flush as their skin reddens across their chest, shoulders and arms, Others have nipple erections, as women do - and nipple stimulation can be another source of pleasure for him. Sweating during or after orgasm is quite common, but this can be profuse and not directly related to the physical effort that has gone into lovemaking.

The skin of the scrotum thickens and retracts, and there is an increasing urge for further stimulation of the penis. When arousal reaches a certain point near to climax, a man reaches the 'point of no return' and cannot hold back his ejaculation. During orgasm, there is a rhythmic throbbing of the penis as semen is pumped out. The penis then becomes limp again and it can take some time for a man to be ready for re-arousal.

After orgasm, many men feel tired, both physically and mentally, and tend to want to go to sleep. They are usually also resistant to any further sexual stimulation which can feel irritating, sore, or even painful.

Woman's Arousal

The body changes in a woman when she is aroused are in some ways similar to those in a man. Although the average woman usually takes longer to become aroused, she remains aroused longer and (unlike a man) can be capable of almost instant re-arousal. Also, women tend not to be as easily aroused by visual stimuli alone; they respond more to romance and intimacy.

(1) As a woman becomes aroused her outer lips swell and open up, revealing the inner lips which also swell and darken.

(2) The vagina begins to moisten.

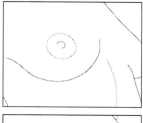

(3) Her breasts in their normal state.

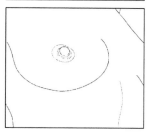

(4) Then begin to swell; her nipples erect and the aureola - the darker ring of skin around the nipple - grows smaller.

As excitement begins, a woman's nipples erect and her breasts swell. As more blood flows in, there may be a sex flush over her chest and neck, her lips redden and she begins to sweat slightly. The vagina becomes moist as a lubricating fluid is produced by its walls, to ease penetration by the penis. The genitals swell and darken as they fill with blood, especially around the inner lips. The outer lips also swell and open up, and the vagina becomes progressively more moist.

Stimulation of the clitoris makes it erect, although the response is not always as quick as with penile erection. The clitoris can also become erect if other sexually-sensitive parts of the body such as the breasts or the vagina are stimulated, but again the response can be much slower than that in a man.

As sexual tension grows, the vagina balloons at its top end and the clitoris may seem to disappear as it retracts inside its hood. Orgasm occurs when there are intense contractions of the pelvic muscles and uterus. Some women's bodies may go into a sort of spasm; they may groan or cry out, and gasp or bite their lip as the sensations flood through them, while others may have a less noticeable or dramatic response.

After orgasm, it may take between 15 and 30 minutes for the body to return to normal, and (again, unlike men) most women welcome some form of loving behaviour during this period.

Multiple Orgasms

One difference between men's and women's sexuality is that some women are capable of having more than one orgasm during a single bout of lovemaking. While a man involuntarily returns quickly to the resting stage after orgasm, some women can remain in a highly aroused state and, with further stimulation, reach orgasm again and again. Others, however, can find the sensation of further stimulation too intense and even painful after they have had their first orgasm.

Simultaneous Orgasms

Some couples at times aim to achieve simultaneous orgasms as the goal of lovemaking. Although it can be extremely pleasurable, it should not become the aim of every session, or even many. Certainly, enjoying each other's orgasms is a major aspect of a loving sexual relationship, so going for simultaneous orgasm can be worth trying for occasionally when it feels right. But if it becomes the sole goal of lovemaking, it may lead to disappointment and even resentment. If going for simultaneous orgasms ever starts to detract from you having pleasurable sex, it makes sense to leave it, at least for a while.

In most cases the man will have to slow down his orgasm and the woman speed hers up. Extended foreplay and a high-level arousal for the woman is probably the first step. Choose a position in which she can control the rhythm, position and depth of penetration; any position that allows manual stimulation of her clitoris by either of you will help. Slowing down a man is slightly more difficult, but positions in which the man is lying on his back will tend to delay his response. You can also use the squeeze technique (see Chapter Four).

One unfortunate side-effect of simultaneous orgasm can be that, even if both of you climax at the same time, it may not necessarily be pleasurable for either of you. A man trying to hold back his ejaculation can lose his timing and much of his pleasure, and the same can be true for the woman who tries to hurry hers. It is important, however, for both partners to continue to let each other know, by general body language, sounds or words, how close they are to climaxing.

UNDERSTANDING YOURSELF

Not every lovemaking session has to end in orgasm, let alone simultaneous orgasm. It can be the natural outcome of lovemaking, but there are times when all sorts of factors, such as tiredness, alcohol or medications may preclude achieving it.

For some women, too, achieving or enjoying orgasm can be more complicated, or subtle, than for men. With practice, and willingness to be open with your partner, it is possible to make real progress towards more reliable and more pleasurable orgasms for her.

Learn to relax with your own body, appreciate it, discover what feels nice about it, and let yourself go with your feelings. Masturbate to intimately discover your own bodily sensations both aroused and unaroused - and get to know what you like to do and where you would like to be touched by your partner. Watch your partner masturbate and learn what he or she likes best. Try to share your innermost feelings and experiences with your partner: you will come to realize how similar they are in many ways, and how you can learn and benefit from your differences. A couple who are intimate out of bed are also invariably closer in bed.

It is easy to think that good sex centres on the genitals and, because of that, to miss out on the pleasures that can be derived from other parts of our own and our partner's body.

DISCOVER EACH OTHER

Enjoy exploring and arousing your partner's body slowly and thoroughly. Stimulate them by using different forms of touch, such as kisses, nibbles or licking: stroke them lightly, then firmly. Don't just caress with hands but try using your hair, breasts or penis. Take things slowly, and really begin to learn which parts of your partner's body gives them most pleasure. Spend time finding out what kind of stimulation is the most exciting for each of you. The important thing is always to let your lover know what pleases you - perhaps with a sigh of pleasure — and for your partner to show the enjoyment that they should be feeling from seeing you so excited.

His Erogenous Zones

Erogenous zones are the parts of the body that provide sexual excitement when touched or stroked but excitement can be even more intense if these zones are kissed, licked or touched with the tongue. Although the genitals are the most sensitive areas of a man's or woman's body, many other areas can produce intense sexual sensations if stimulated properly. The best way to discover your partner's pleasure zones is through foreplay and especially during sensual massage.

Generally, a man's body is less sensitive than a woman's with only some areas of his body producing erotic feelings when stroked, caressed or kissed. They include:

- Any area of the face and neck, but in particular the lips, respond sensually to touch and kissing.

- Shoulders, back, chest and nipples will all provide pleasurable sensations if stroked. Sucking a man's nipples will often make them erect and become more sensitive to further stimulation.

- A man's buttocks can provide sensual feelings. There's no need to be gentle here - quite firm kneading provides the most pleasurable results.

- When massaged, his hands, fingertips and the soles of his feet can all provide erotic stimulation.

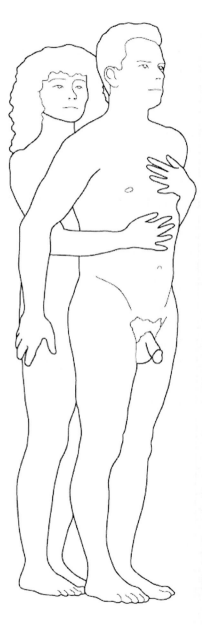

UNDERSTANDING EACH OTHER

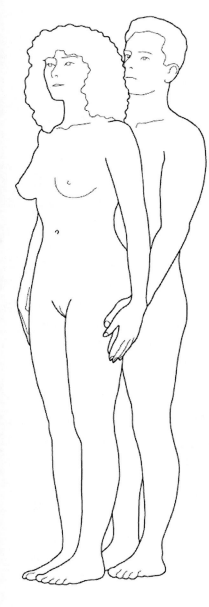

Her Erogenous Zones

Some would say that, in contrast, the whole of a woman's body is an erogenous zone, to a greater or lesser extent, and that all of her skin can be responsive to stimulation by hands, mouth or tongue.

- Try light touches on the cheeks, eyelids, eyebrows, forehead and along the hairline. Kisses on the back of the neck and the earlobes, can have electric results.

- A woman's mouth, when stimulated by her lover's mouth or fingertips, can directly affect her entire body and in particular her nipples and genitals.

- Arms, armpits and hands may all respond to sensual touching.

- Her back, hips and abdomen - especially around the navel - respond to light touches or kisses.

- Feet and legs can produce pleasure for a woman when stroked; the insides of her thighs and backs of her knees can also produce highly arousing sensations when they are kissed.

- A woman's breasts and nipples can be highly sensitive and for about half of women play a prime part in their sexual arousal. Stroking, kissing, sucking or gently nibbling can produce sensational effects.

- Buttocks are rich in nerves and can be stimulated by kneading, rubbing patting or even gentle slapping.

- Stroking or kissing the perineum can be highly pleasurable.

QUESTION TIME

Q. I think our sex life is okay. We make love three or four times a week and both always climax. But my partner complains that she doesn't really enjoy our lovemaking that much - not like she used to when we first knew each other. Why?

A. You are right to be concerned and take the responsibility of making things better. If the aim of your lovemaking is only geared to producing orgasms, it could be lacking the intimacy that makes sex special. It's time to make an effort outside the bedroom as well.

The emotional side of a relationship is as important as the physical side. Make a plan to go back to your original courtship behaviour, spend more time talking and have the occasional romantic evening together, either out or at home. Even better, if you can, take her on a romantic holiday and take the time to rediscover each other.

Q. We've never had simultaneous orgasms even though we've tried occasionally. Is there something we are doing wrong?

A. Firstly, if trying for simultaneous orgasms is giving neither of you any pleasure, then it is best to stop trying. It can happen from time to time anyway. Generally, if you do want to climax together, you will probably have to speed up the woman's response and slow down the man's. Extended foreplay using both hands and mouth to arouse the woman is usually necessary, while only little stimulation of the man's genitals should slow down his ejaculatory urge.

Another way to slow down the man is to choose a woman-on-top position, or one that allows deep penetration where the head of his penis receives less stimulation.

There are many people, however, who find non-synchronised orgasms far more rewarding. The fact that one partner puts his or her energy into pleasing the other, which is then reciprocated, emphasises the giving and receiving which is the cornerstone of a loving relationship.

Q. I've always been worried that my penis is rather small. Will this affect my ability to provide orgasms for my partner?

A. No. Penis size is one of the big male hang ups. The fact is that virtually every vagina will accommodate a penis of any size and be stimulated in the same way. Many women claim that the length of the penis has no effect whatsoever; and, that it is the girth that is more important. The main problem for a man who thinks that he has a small penis can be that he acts like someone who thinks that he has a small penis.

Q. I have read that some women have more than one orgasm when they have sex, but I've never had more than one. Am I unusual?

A. No, many women naturally stop at one. Some women are able to have multiple orgasms by continued stimulation after the first orgasm. These women remain at the plateau stage of arousal rather than entering the resolution phase and, from there, can repeatedly achieve orgasm.

During intercourse a lot may depend on your partner. He will need to need to hold back from his orgasm in order to maintain his erection, and therefore to prolong lovemaking for you. A great many women report that the only way they can achieve multiple orgasms is through masturbation. Women who are capable of multiple orgasms do not have them every time they make love, nor do they, necessarily, want to. There is probably no reason whatsoever to stop you having as many orgasms as you like, provided that stimulation continues for long enough and is of the right kind.

CHAPTER TWO
KISSING AND CARESSING

Foreplay, masturbation and oral sex can be pleasures in themselves, and they can be important preliminaries to varied, exciting and fulfilling lovemaking.

FOREPLAY

Before I met Mal, I can't really remember having any proper orgasms. It didn't bother me then, as I was still having a good time. Or so I thought. I suppose it's what you're used to, and what you don't know you don't miss. But from the very beginning with him, I knew that things were different. For a start, we spent a lot more time kissing and petting, which was something the other men I'd slept with weren't much interested in. All they wanted was to grab my breasts, then dive straight in and have sex. Somehow Mal seemed to know when and where to touch me, and, for the first time, I felt sensations deep in my body that I hadn't felt before. Sometimes, he stimulates me until I climax before penetration; other times it's not long after he does finally slip himself into me that I have these incredibly powerful orgasms.

Fiona

Foreplay implies that it has to come before something else, but it doesn't have to. It can be a delicious and rewarding pleasure in its own right; there is no reason at all why sex should always involve intercourse. One technique in the art of prolonged foreplay is to avoid the genital areas for as long as you can, as you build up the excitement.

Because men are more easily aroused than women, they often rush too quickly into genital contact and penetration, ignoring the fact that a woman generally needs some time to become fully aroused. A sensitive man will try to control his impulses and take time to arouse his partner, gradually building up her excitement with all sorts of kisses and caresses before he moves on to stimulating her breasts and genitals.

Extended foreplay is exciting for both partners: the man can achieve a firmer erection whilst the woman becomes more moist, more receptive to intercourse and, as a result, more likely to achieve her orgasm.

Kissing, caressing and cuddling are all potent stimuli that trigger the release of sex hormones into the bloodstream. As these circulate, they act on a part of the brain which sends signals to release even more arousal hormones.

Whether you are with a new partner or in a long-standing relationship,
do not neglect the pleasures of foreplay. Building up the excitement gradually,
by kissing and caressing each other, even before you undress completely,
only serves to heighten the pleasures to come.

Kissing

Sex shouldn't be solely confined to the bedroom. Foreplay and other pleasures can start long before you get there. Our first physical encounter with a partner is usually prolonged kissing – a vastly enjoyable activity that can often be overlooked later in an established relationship. In fact, when relationships go wrong, it is usually the case that the kissing stops before intercourse does.

Try not to start with too much activity. Begin slowly and gently, with your lips relishing the contact. Try not to let your kisses be too wet or slobbery. Do not ram your tongue instantly into your partner's mouth or down their throat. Tease a little by kissing other parts of your partner's face - the forehead, eyelids, cheeks, as you draw your lips across them. Let the passion grow slowly and delicately. Try running your tongue around your partner's teeth and, as the excitement builds, push it further into the mouth. You can fence with each other's tongues, or imitate the motions of sexual intercourse by thrusting your tongue in and out of one another's mouths.

Kissing does not need to be restricted to the mouth. Kisses on the earlobes, neck, throat and shoulders, or nibbling, or even gentle biting, can be highly erotic. Try kissing and sucking fingers and toes and watching the response. Explore every part of your lover's body, even those you think may not respond. Breasts are usually highly sensitive and should be approached gently, to start with. Usually only when a woman is aroused will a firmer touch, and kissing, sucking and gentle nibbling of her nipples be pleasurable.

Many men, too, enjoy having their nipples caressed, licked and kissed. Go all over your partner's body, first with kisses then with the tip of your tongue. Be tantalising and only reach the genitals for perhaps the most intimate kisses of all late in the arousal process. Gently nibble and suck – or first wet and then blow on – particularly sensitive parts of your partner's body; the pleasures of giving can be as great as those of receiving.

The gentle touch

Combine kissing with caressing and stroking your partner's body all over, first gently, and then building up the pressure as the excitement mounts. As with kissing, to build arousal take time to reach caressing each other's genitals and begin by concentrating on other parts of your partner's body. Both men and women, for example, enjoy having their buttocks stroked, squeezed or kneaded, and even gently smacked. A finger run lightly around the anal area can also create exquisite sensations.

Use all your body to tease and to rub up against your partner. The woman can use her breasts, nipples or hair to run over the man's body, to create sensations quite unlike those given by hands and fingers. The man can use his penis and scrotum in almost the same way, pleasuring her by drawing them gently across the most sensitive parts of her body.

All men enjoy having their penis gripped, and most enjoy having their testicles held, or even gently squeezed; a woman may want to avoid stimulating the man's genitals for too long, or too energetically, before she is really ready for penetration, though, as extensive stimulation of this kind will often be enough to bring a man to climax.

The man should ensure that genital caresses of his partner are not too excessive before she is properly aroused, when they may be more irritating and sore-making, rather than exciting. Don't rush her. The first touches should be gentle and, though she should begin self-lubricating, you could help by using a commercial lube or nature's own saliva. You can then begin building up the pressure and movement as she nears her orgasm – but always be guided by her.

(1) Explore every part of your lover's body, concentrating on the areas that you know give the most pleasure, but avoid the genitals for as long as possible until you are either happy for one or both of you to climax or ready for intercourse. Use your own body, your hands, mouth and tongue to provide sensual feelings for your partner, and all the time be guided by watching each other's expressions and listening to the sounds of pleasure.

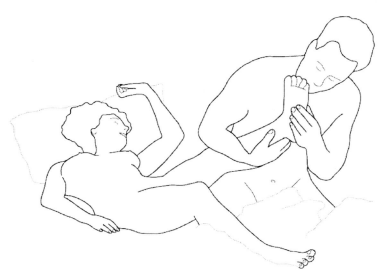

(2) To build arousal, do not always concentrate your caresses on the most obvious parts of the body too soon. Massaging feet or hands, for example, can have a wonderfully relaxing and erotic effect. The art of successful lovemaking is to take as much time as you need, or wish.

I used to think that the quicker I could enter Maxine the better it was for me. But she showed me that there was a whole range of other sensations that I could enjoy, too. When she brushes my nipples with her lips, or runs her fingers gently between my balls and bum, I don't want the feelings to stop, even though my erection seems to be bursting. Now, I like to hold back as long as I can when she fondles me, and I can really say that when I climax it is better than ever.

Jason

KISSING AND CARESSING

Undressing as foreplay

Undressing provocatively can be an exciting part of foreplay. Revealing their body, or their partner's body in a tantalising way can be a turn on for both men and women. It has long been thought that most men respond much more quickly to visual stimuli than women. For both, though, a hint of nudity can often have a stronger effect than complete nakedness. Slowly removing clothes as a show for one another should always be a turn on for you both.

If a man or woman is confident enough to strip for his or her lover, this can be highly erotic for the recipient as they can take the passive role in the proceedings for a while. For those men who feel that they always have to initiate sex, this will be particularly arousing.

Try undressing each other, then each of you can show off your bodies without feeling required to take any further initiative for a while. You do not have to remove all of your clothes to make love; both men and women can find it highly enjoyable if their partner retains a piece of sexy underwear or even, say, a shirt, to heighten the sense of spontaneity and tease.

Erotic materials

It can be fun to experiment with different sensations of touch during foreplay. Try using a range of different materials, fur or feathers, for example, across each other's bodies. Ice can also have an electric effect when it is run across the skin, and even the genitals (make sure, though, that it's slightly melting as it can stick to the skin and burn if straight from the freezer).

MASTURBATION

When we first started living together and then got married, I just never would have thought of masturbating. I would have felt it was a kind of betrayal, you know. Then, he went on this training course to do with work, and he was away for a week and one morning, well it just sort of happened. Then I thought, why not? It's such a release and there's no one else involved. Anyway, I usually fantasise about him so it's a kind of compliment. He's now got promotion and has to travel quite a lot and I still masturbate when he's away. But now I find that I also do it when he's here. It doesn't mean that I enjoy sex with him any less or that I prefer masturbation. The way I see it, it's an extension of my sex life with him. Actually, sometimes the better sex is with him, the more I want to bring myself off as well, do you see that? It's just totally different from anything we do together - unless, of course, I'm doing it in front of him. He likes me to do that too sometimes.

Nicky

Contrary to what many may want to believe, or have been told, masturbation is not something that does, or should, stop when two people become involved in a loving sexual relationship. Research shows that nearly all men, and most women, continue to masturbate throughout their active sexual lives. It should not be seen as a solitary activity, implying lonely sexual frustration, but a continuing source of self-pleasure, development and a safe release. It helps you understand your own sexual responses, is only harmful in major excess, keeps everything in working order, expands your fantasy life, and it can help you sleep.

Watching each other

Mutual masturbation is a great way to learn how to give each other pleasure as part of extended foreplay. The only way to really learn how best to masturbate your partner is to watch them doing it. Note how hands and fingers are used, which areas appear to be more sensitive, your partner's breathing and sounds of pleasure. If you are happy to, it can be worth talking about what you have learned, whilst you kiss and cuddle each other afterwards.

Although you may find it difficult or embarrassing at first, showing rather than just telling will have real benefits. Using what you learn to please each other, you can aim to masturbate your partner as well as they do themselves, if not better.

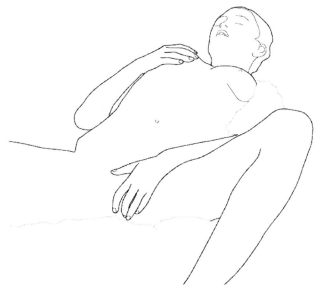

(1) When women masturbate, they may use stimuli that change as they become more excited.

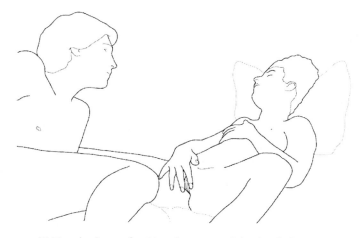

(2) Note the change of position of your partner's hand as she brings herself to climax - how she stimulates her outer lips.

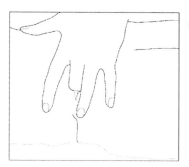

(3) If and when she inserts a finger.

(4) Or the pressure and rhythm she uses on her clitoris.

The woman

Women often start masturbating slowly, and build up movement, rhythm and pressure gradually. Watch her initial speed and rhythm, how many fingers she uses, what parts of her body she stimulates most. Women, unlike men, do not always mimic the actions of intercourse, or of a penis thrusting in and out; they use a pattern of stimuli, and not always aimed directly at producing an orgasm. Many women concentrate on stimulating the clitoris alone – and by rubbing, tugging or even tapping it. Some women may stimulate only the vaginal lips, and some may insert one finger or maybe more.

Observe the speed, pressures and rhythms as she reaches her arousal plateau: many women at this stage prefer a steady rhythm. This is particularly important, as women often say that men do not maintain the right rhythm and pressure at the crucial time.

The main thing to learn is that everyone has their preferences, and that everyone is unique. Movements can be circular or up and down; pressure can be hard or soft or a combination of the two at different times; some women like tapping the clitoris with a finger or two. Watch where she puts her other hand if she is not using both. Does she caress her breasts, or thighs? Many women enjoy more than just the direct stimulation of the genital area. By watching their partner's actions and getting further guidance, most men can learn the art of masturbating a woman to help her achieve her orgasm.

The man

I remember in the early stages of our relationship Alan once said "You're not doing it right" and I just said, "Well do it yourself" – and he did! I was shocked at first, even a little hurt, but then it was just fascinating to watch. The whole way he handled it was different – I suppose I found out quite a lot. Then one time we were just about to make love and I asked him if he'd like to see me touch myself. When he said yes, I was suddenly unsure, but began to relax when I saw how much it turned him on.

Sue

Generally, most men tend to masturbate in the same way. Their aim is to re-create the movements of intercourse so they encircle the penis with one hand and pump up and down. The rim around the head, or glans, of the penis and and the bridge of skin underneath the head between it and the shaft, the frenum, are stimulated by the thumb and index finger. How hard a man grips is up to him. As his orgasm approaches his hand movements may become more rapid but, as he ejaculates, the pumping action usually slows down considerably or even stops, as the head of the penis becomes very sensitive at this stage, and over-vigorous stimulation can be painful.

The main things to look for as you watch the man masturbate are the position of his hand and the location of his thumb and fingers on his penis. Note the type of strokes he makes. Are they long or short, slow or jerky? Look out for changes in his body as he nears orgasm. Do his penis, scrotum and testicles undergo any changes? Learn to

KISSING AND CARESSING

recognise the appearance of any pre-ejaculatory fluid – a usually transparent lubricant which precedes the ejaculation of semen; it can indicate how aroused he is. What does he do with his other hand at the moment of ejaculation? Does he stimulate other parts of his body such as his scrotum, nipples or anus? Most importantly, note when he stops stimulating himself and any changes that occur as he relaxes.

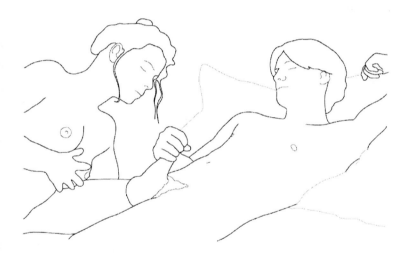

When the man begins to masturbate, his partner should note how he holds his penis and what he does with his other hand as he becomes more excited. As he nears orgasm, look for changes in the speed, rhythm and grip of his hands. Watch the expression on his face so you can know when he is about to climax.

Touching each other

After a few sessions of watching each other masturbate, you should have learned a lot. Choose a comfortable position - one in which you will not tire too easily. It makes sense, if you are right-handed, to be on your partner's right, for example.

Touching him

The main thing is to hold the shaft of the penis quite firmly, just below the head; a loose grip can be more frustrating than enjoyable. There is a variety of ways to hold the penis - she can use the finger and thumb ring technique, or grasp it with the whole hand; she can even try rolling the penis between her hands or against her thigh like dough. Whatever you do, try to make sure your hand does not get tired. Change hands if it does. Ask your partner what feels good and try to replicate what you have learned from watching him masturbate.

If he is circumcised you are likely to need plenty of lubricant to prevent him getting sore.

For more exotic masturbation, try using both hands so the entire penis is encased. Or try wrapping your hair, fur, feathers – or even a string of pearls - around his penis. One of the most delicious forms of masturbation for a man is to have his penis gripped between your breasts.

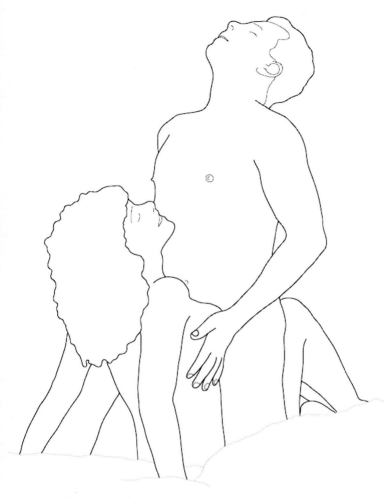

For a man, perhaps the most delicious form of masturbation is to
have his penis gripped between the woman's breasts.

Touching her

Hannah's brought herself to orgasm in front of me a couple of times now, and I've learned so much. I've learned how to tickle her clitoris and how she likes to push down on her pubis. I also realised I was rubbing too hard and too fast. So now when I touch her slowly and softly, she not only enjoys it more, but I relax, knowing that I'm doing the right thing.

Ian

The man masturbating a woman must remember that the clitoris is a very delicate organ and should be treated gently, especially at first. His fingers should be lubricated with saliva, or vaginal fluid, as the whole genital area is sensitive to friction. Be guided by your partner, but generally a woman prefers fairly gentle pressure at first, only building up as she nears orgasm. Stimulation of the clitoris can be direct or indirect, but do not apply direct pressure unless your partner enjoys it.

Start by putting your whole hand over the vulva and making either circular or vibrating movements. Be guided by what she likes best. As she becomes more aroused, try inserting a finger into her vagina and moving it slowly in and out as you stimulate her clitoris. Don't be afraid to let her guide your hand and fingers to exactly the spot she likes best. And all the while do not forget to stimulate her breasts and other parts of her body. When she reaches orgasm do not stop stimulating her clitoris: some women need continued clitoral excitement during orgasm. Ask her what she likes.

When you have learned how your partner masturbates, it is time to take turns to masturbate each other. Using what you have learned, try to masturbate your partner as well as they do themselves – and maybe even better...

When both of you are confident that you can masturbate one another well, try masturbating each other at the same time. Choose a position in which you are both comfortable, and take it in turns to bring each other to orgasm or, with a little practice, perhaps to simultaneous orgasm.

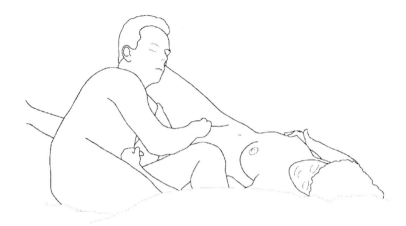

When you have learned how to masturbate each other well,
it is time to try masturbating each other at the same time.

ORAL SEX

*It might have been shyness that stopped us rushing into having oral
sex. Sally seemed worried about me ejaculating in her mouth, and
that I would dislike her taste, or her smell. Well, we both decided
that the best thing to do was to take it gradually, until it felt right to
try it. Once she had tasted my semen, she said it wasn't as bad as she
had imagined, which was a relief. And far from disliking her taste,
not only do I love it, but I have found one of the greatest sensations
of all - her having vaginal spasms wrapped around my tongue.*

Pete

Licking or sucking your partner's genitals is, to most people, the most intimate thing you can do together in a sexual relationship. The act demonstrates an enormous amount of trust, not only because it can be painful for either partner if not done carefully, but also because it shows a deep level of acceptance of each other, far more than in any other type of lovemaking. For many couples, oral sex is simply an extension of sensual foreplay and a prelude to intercourse, while for others it can be an occasional main route to orgasm.

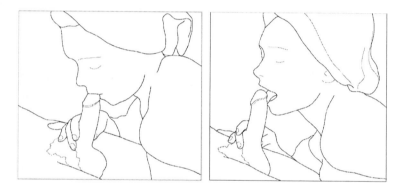

Oral sex often happens best as the last of a series of kisses all over your partner's body.
For the woman who is giving, run your tongue over the head, or glans, of the man's penis, pushing it into the small slit at the tip, or urethra. Next, swirl your tongue around the rim of the head and vibrate it against the ridge at the back, or frenum.

Barriers to enjoying oral sex are nearly always in the mind. You may worry about your genital odour or taste, but there is nothing that attention to hygiene and daily bathing or showering can't deal with. Try taking a bath together; washing each other as part of foreplay can be very sensual as well as allaying any fears. In fact nearly all men find the taste of the slightly acid vaginal juices perfectly enjoyable and some find it one of the greatest taste sensations.

Many women are apprehensive about their partner ejaculating in her mouth. You may want to agree beforehand if this is not what you want. The man can then signal when he feels the urge to climax, and then withdraw. His partner can continue to masturbate him to orgasm or move on to intercourse. A woman who is unsure about swallowing semen can always begin by finishing him by hand. She can also try spitting it out, if she is happy to try getting used to the taste and volume of her lover's ejaculation.

Some women might also worry about choking if the penis is thrust too deeply into their mouth. This is easy for her to control, though, by gripping the shaft of the penis to limit how much of it she takes into her mouth. Another ploy is to use your hand to direct his penis at your cheek and not down your throat. However he is positioned, the man should not thrust too vigorously, especially when he reaches the point when he is about to climax.

For a man, having his penis sucked or licked can be the ultimate in eroticism and probably the most powerful sexual stimulus he can have. To him, the mouth feels like a different, animated, vagina; his partner's tongue stimulating the sensitive parts of his penis's head giving him strong extra sensations.

For a woman, having her vaginal area, and particularly her clitoris, kissed, or licked, can be equally exciting. Although the tongue cannot penetrate the vagina very deeply, it is capable of more varied stimulation than a man's fingers or penis, and has a much softer, and obviously wetter feel. By using his tongue and lips together a man can provide highly arousing sensations to the clitoral and vaginal area at the same time. Very sophisticated oral sensations can be had if the man wraps his lips around the clitoris and sucks upon it; it can be delicious to vary this with fast strumming of the clitoris with the tip of the tongue.

Teeth are sharp and the genitals sensitive, so try to cover your teeth with your lips and be careful not to bite even if you become very excited. Also, never blow into your lover's genitals – this can be dangerous for both partners as it can force air into the bloodstream – with serious consequences.

From her to him

Choose a relaxing and comfortable position at first, such as your partner lying down on his back or his side. Or, for something different – and you are happy not to see it as submissive but giving - he can stand while you kneel in front of him, or he can sit in a chair or on the edge of the bed. Whatever position you choose, keep his penis pointing upwards as it can be painful for him if you pull it down too far when you are sucking.

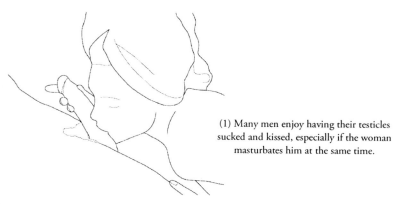

(1) Many men enjoy having their testicles sucked and kissed, especially if the woman masturbates him at the same time.

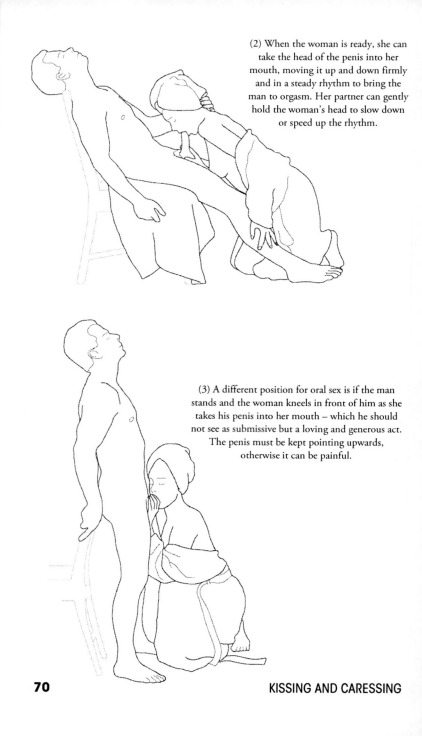

(2) When the woman is ready, she can take the head of the penis into her mouth, moving it up and down firmly and in a steady rhythm to bring the man to orgasm. Her partner can gently hold the woman's head to slow down or speed up the rhythm.

(3) A different position for oral sex is if the man stands and the woman kneels in front of him as she takes his penis into her mouth – which he should not see as submissive but a loving and generous act. The penis must be kept pointing upwards, otherwise it can be painful.

KISSING AND CARESSING

Begin by kissing other parts of your lover's body before moving on to his genitals. Kiss and lick the inside of his thighs, and remember that his scrotum is also very sensitive. Tease him slightly while gently masturbating him, then gradually move down towards his penis. Start to kiss and lick it, then hold the shaft firmly and run your tongue across the head, pressing your tongue into the hole.

Next, run your tongue around the ridge between the head and the shaft of the penis and flick your tongue against the frenum. Try licking the length of the shaft of the penis as if it were an ice lolly, and trip your tongue over the ridge. Play with any combination of these movements until you are ready to take his penis into your mouth.

Keep your teeth covered with your lips and gently take the glans into your mouth. There is a whole range of sensations that you can now create for your partner. Sucking, using your tongue on the shaft or head, strumming on the ridge of skin (frenum) behind the head or pushing his penis in and out of your mouth will all create different pleasurable effects. As you become more confident about oral sex you can experiment with other movements and sensations.

Use your hands to stimulate other sensitive parts of his body, such as his nipples and buttocks, while you are sucking him to build up the excitement, A finger run lightly around his anal area, or, well-lubricated and inserted shallowly into his anus – or even as far as his G-Spot, if that's what you are both happy with – can create delicious orgasms for him.

To bring your partner to orgasm, move your mouth up and down his penis in a steady rhythm, making sure that you keep a firm pressure, As long as he doesn't become too controlling, you could choose to let him guide you by placing his hands on your head so he can slow you down or speed you up as he feels the need. As your speed increases, he will reach the brink of orgasm, so hold the shaft with one hand if you do not want him to thrust too deeply, and help him to withdraw if you do not want him to ejaculate in your mouth.

From him to her

Mostly, women prefer oral sex to build up gradually. Start kissing her all over her body and then move on. Probably the best position is for the woman to lie on her back, with her legs apart and her hips slightly raised on a pillow, so that the man can easily reach every part of her genitals.

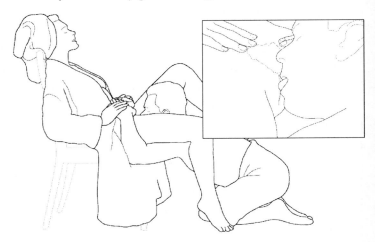

(1) In the "from him to her" situation, the woman can sit on a chair, or on the edge of the bed, so that her partner has better access to every part of her genitals. He can easily reach her clitoris and can insert his tongue into the entrance of her vagina to mimic the motion of intercourse.

KISSING AND CARESSING

(2) Another exciting variation is for the woman to sit over her partner's face while he uses his tongue and lips to stimulate her. One advantage is that the woman has a certain amount of control and can direct the man's tongue to where she likes it best.

The insides of a woman's thighs can be particularly sensitive, so begin by kissing and gently licking there as a hint of what is to come, Kiss her pubis, first gently then more firmly, before you run your tongue along the outer lips. Part them gently with your tongue, gradually running it up towards her clitoris. She may like you to part her lips with your fingers and thrust your tongue in and out of her vagina – to simulate the movements of your penis when you make love. All sorts of variations are possible. Try swirling your tongue in a regular rhythm around the entrance to her vagina, using a firm lower lip to rub her pubis, gently tugging at her vaginal lips with your mouth, sucking her clitoris as it erects. After some sessions of oral sex, and a few experiments, the man should learn what his partner likes best.

Many women need direct stimulation of their clitoris to have an orgasm. Be firm but gentle, as the clitoris is sensitive and can become very tender. Vibrating your tongue against the clitoris, keeping a steady but accelerating rhythm, can be the best way to bring your partner to orgasm. But be guided by her. As she nears her climax, she may make pelvic movements to direct the speed and pressure that she wants, so try to keep your head steady and let her push against you. During all this time caress her body, particularly her breasts and buttocks, to give her maximum pleasure.

There are many variations to try. A rear-entry approach can be difficult at first for the man to reach the clitoris, but this can be overcome with practice. A big turn on for many couples is for the woman to sit over the man's mouth and direct her vagina and clitoris onto his tongue. The feeling of the woman being in charge can be extremely exciting.

I'm sure a lot of people worry about oral sex. There's no need! You really have to know someone well and care about them, but then when you do it there's nothing to beat it. It is wonderfully erotic and also such a commitment to each other that everything you do sexually afterwards is that much more special.

Maria

Giving and taking

Many people believe that the ultimate in oral sex is the position everyone talks about, the one known as 69, where you give and receive simultaneously. Whether the man or the woman is on top, or you are side by side, this position can be extremely exciting and arousing but it can have drawbacks.

Some men say that they find it difficult to stimulate their partner properly from this angle. It is also essential to keep a degree of control because, while letting go at the moment of climax, you may inadvertently bite your partner. Not a good move!

As with all sexual activity, everyone will find out what suits them best. There is rarely an entirely right or wrong way to do it.

The celebrated 69 position is often regarded as the ultimate in oral sex.
It does, however, need a certain amount of practice to make it satisfactory
for both partners. In this position you can either take it in turns to climax,
or try for simultaneous orgasms. But be careful not to bite your partner's
genitals in the ecstasy of climaxing.

QUESTION TIME

Q: When my lover masturbates me before we have intercourse, he makes it feel good to begin with, but then somehow it all goes wrong and I lose the feeling of wanting to climax. Is there anything I can do?

A: You can show him exactly how you masturbate yourself to orgasm, the way you change the pressure and rhythm of your hand, and the parts of your genitals that you stimulate as your arousal increases. For men, masturbation usually mimics the motions of intercourse, while for women there can be a whole pattern of stimuli that are used. It may be difficult for men to realise this, unless they are helped by their partner, when they are usually only too pleased to be shown how to give maximum pleasure.

Q: I want to give my partner oral sex but I am really worried about him ejaculating in my mouth. What can I do?

A: You can simply agree beforehand that he will not do this. He should signal to you when he is about to climax and then you can remove his penis from your mouth. A common fear for women is that the volume of semen will be too much to swallow, and that it will taste unpleasant. Actually, the average man only ejaculates about 10cc, or the volume of a sugar cube. It is worthwhile watching him come separately to see exactly how much there is.

The taste is slightly salty – some women compare its taste and consistency to oysters. If you do not want to swallow, you can easily remove your mouth as he comes, or take it into your mouth and discreetly spit it out. Do talk to your partner about how you feel and decide together on how you are going to proceed.

Q: We have a really active sex life, but sometimes I still masturbate even when my partner is around. Am I unusual?

A: Most men, and many women, continue to masturbate throughout their active sexual lives, even in a permanent relationship. Very often, the better the sex together, the more people masturbate, as there is a constant high level of sexual arousal.

As many people fantasise about their partner when they masturbate, it very often helps to strengthen the relationship.

Another bonus is that the release of orgasm during masturbation can take the pressure off needing, or wanting, to have intercourse at every opportunity. You both have more time to talk and be affectionate to each other before you jump into bed – all things that create the intimacy that sustains a loving relationship.

Q: When my boyfriend kisses me I just feel so sexy. My nipples erect and my vagina gets wet almost immediately. I'm worried that I'm oversexed if that's all it takes to get me going.

A: You are not by any means oversexed – just reacting naturally to your erotic feelings. For both men and women – but particularly women – the mouth and lips are highly erogenous zones as they are full of sensitive nerve endings. For a woman, a particularly sensitive and erotic kiss can instigate sensual responses throughout her entire body. Unfortunately, too many men forget this and try to go for caressing a woman's breasts and genitals right away. Kissing, holding hands, caressing almost any part of the body that is not obviously associated with sex, can show loving and caring in a far more intimate way and can often trigger very strong arousal responses.

CHAPTER THREE
MAKING LOVE

Better lovemaking for greater pleasure.

How different positions can increase sensual enjoyment.

BETTER SEX

When we first started to have sex I think we tried every position we could think of in those first few months. After a while, you get to know which ones suit you both, which give the most pleasure and stimulation. I could tell what Phil liked best from his face, or by the way his body reacted to certain things. His favourite is the doggie position which gives very deep penetration. It also allows him to reach around to caress my breasts and clitoris. My favourite is being on top so that I can set the pace and rhythm, in fact be completely in charge, and, more important, to see all his responses.

Sabrina

While masturbation and oral sex can be wholly satisfying forms of sexual activity in themselves – whether they are used as prolonged love-play and end in orgasm – penetrative sex is still seen as the culmination of sexual activity by most people.

Most couples, in the early stage of their relationship, experiment with many different positions and eventually settle down to a few favourite ones. Some positions may be used only occasionally, depending on how a couple feel. Others will use several positions during one lovemaking session. One may be enormously exciting for one partner but not for the other, and each may need to be in a different position to achieve orgasm. Nobody becomes an expert immediately; it usually takes a few months before you begin properly to discover what you both like best.

Penetration

Different positions create different sensations. One of major importance is the angle at which the penis enters the vagina and the depth to which it penetrates. Generally, when a woman has her legs straight, penetration is at its shallowest and when they are drawn back, at its deepest. By altering the angle of her legs, a woman can make the man's penis come into contact with different parts of her vagina and thus affect where there is the most stimulation. Very deep penetration can be achieved if the woman is on all fours, in a doggie position, and this also allows the penis to stimulate the area around her G-spot.

Sex at its best involves quite a lot of movement, and certain positions are preferable depending on who wants to do most of the moving. A man who wants an orgasm during intercourse will need to experience some penile movement. Most men enjoy thrusting at different speeds and depths, and they usually deepen their thrusting when orgasm is inevitable. All men are different, of course – some go more for short, jerky thrusts; others long, slow ones; and, yet others, a combination – and many man will be attempting to reproduce the movements created during masturbation.

Recent research has found that one of the best ways to stimulate the clitoris during man-on-top intercourse is to adopt a position called CAT, or the Clitoral Alignment Technique. The man rides high up on the woman, his pelvis pressing on the woman's and with her clitoris being ground between the two. The shaft of his penis can now rub towards the top of her vagina. He rests the full weight of his body on his partner, his torso pushing forward towards her head and shoulders. The woman can also wrap her legs around him.

In this position, movement is almost entirely between the pelvic areas of both partners. It is best to establish a rhythm in which the woman leads the upward stroke by forcing the man's pelvis backwards. He allows this to happen while applying counter pressure to her clitoral area. As her pelvis moves forward and upward, his penis enters more deeply.

In the downward stroke the movements are reversed, the man's pelvis pushing the woman's backwards and downwards. She now tries to keep her clitoris in contact by pressing it against his pubic bone. This kind of rocking movement ensures that the penis is also kept close to the clitoris at all times. Maintaining a slow and steady rhythm, without any urgency to reach for orgasm, can produce exquisite climaxes for both. Indeed, many couples claim that orgasms resulting from this technique are the best they have.

Simultaneous orgasms are more common in this position, too.

What women want

Women enjoy the thrusting of the penis, and a man can help his partner achieve a lot of pleasure if he takes his time before going for his own orgasm. Most women say that they prefer slow penetration and a lingering rhythm as their pleasure mounts towards orgasm. There is such a thing, though, as a penis that thrusts too long or too deeply or with insufficient lubrication, which, quite simply, can hurt.

The man can create all kinds of pleasurable sensations for his partner. He can try withdrawing slowly right to the opening of the vagina and tugging at her inner lips with the head of the penis, then teasing her with the tip, alternating his thrusts between deep and shallow, or moving his hips and changing the angle of penetration. He can move his hips to change the angle at which he penetrates and thrust from left and right, or make circular motions with his pelvis. The combinations are endless.

It's true what they say — size doesn't matter! — or, at least, doesn't need to. It's what he does with it. John's really great the way he teases me with his penis. He's always changing the way he thrusts, deep or shallow, or he pushes into me sideways a little or swirls it round inside me. But he's always steady, allowing me to build up slowly but surely and I get these incredible feelings even before I climax.

Miranda

If the woman is on top, she can control the angle, speed and depth of penetration. Rear-entry positions have the advantage of allowing both partners to move freely. If you find a position in which you both have some freedom of movement, try sharing the thrusting movements. The man can withdraw a little and his partner push against his penis and then withdraw a little herself. Go on until orgasm is reached.

A woman could also try contracting the muscles in the vaginal opening, and the deep pelvic muscles, around her partner's penis as it moves inwards, and relaxing them as it moves outwards. This technique is highly stimulating for both partners, and can quickly bring a man to orgasm. The man, meanwhile, could try 'twitching' his penis to reciprocate intriguingly different sensations.

Clitoral stimulation

Women usually need clitoral stimulation to climax. During intercourse the clitoris is stimulated indirectly by the penis as it moves in and out of the vagina: the thrusting movement pulls on the inner lips which are attached to the hood of the clitoris. Many women, however, experience little or no clitoral stimulation from penile thrusting alone and need more direct caresses, perhaps with a hand or even by introducing a vibrator into your lovemaking together.

Different lovemaking positions alter the angle at which the penis enters the vagina and the depth to which it penetrates. By trying different positions, almost every part of the vagina can be stimulated, with correspondingly different sensations for the man's penis as well.

THE FIRST TIME...

When you have sex for the first time, or with a new partner for the first time, the ideal location is somewhere where you can be comfortable and remain undisturbed. Extended foreplay is essential to ensure that the woman is fully aroused and well lubricated before penetration. Take your time if you can and try to resist the temptation to jump into bed straightaway.

Everyone should realise that sex with a partner for the first time does not always turn out to be the magical moment we probably hoped for. There is no reason to worry – indeed, it happens more often than not. Practice improves both performance and satisfaction, and so does knowing what your partner wants or needs. Understanding each other better and the willingness of both people to communicate about their feelings and sexual needs, develops with time.

There are several reasons why things may not work out as we hope the first time we have sex:

Love, lust or just curiosity?

There are many reasons for having sex and each one can influence how your feelings will range between joy and disappointment.

Some people end up in bed together only a few hours after they meet. This can seem great at the time, when the release of orgasm is all they think they need but, afterwards, and particularly for women, recent surveys have shown that they can often feel cheated and dissatisfied and end up with a poorer self-image.

So it can make sense not to rush headlong into sex. For a couple who have known each other for some time, and for whom making love is a way of cementing a close and loving relationship, it can be an ecstatic experience. They will have learned about each other's likes and dislikes. By kissing, cuddling, touching and arousing one another by manual and oral sex, they will have built up a sense of intimacy, and both will have become relaxed and happy in giving and receiving sensual pleasures. For them, penetrative sex becomes just one more step on their sexual journey together, rather than an early, rushed, encounter.

Studies have shown that, before their first time, most boys believed that sex would feel great, while girls expected it to be painful or scary. Even in this day and age, there is a significant percentage of girls who give their boyfriends more access to their bodies than they allow themselves.

Women can enjoy their first sexual intercourse best if they have got to know their own bodies and feel in full control of their sexuality. Often they are the ones who have had a strong and open involvement with their mothers and a good relationship with their fathers. Research reveals that some girls gave their main motivation for having first sex was to please their boyfriend and thus receive affirmation from him of their attractiveness and value. Of course this is not ideal. This kind of affirmation should come from within.

First sex should happen when it can be unhurried and the woman is fully sexually aroused. Some will become wet fairly readily, whilst others may need a fair degree of stimulation to get there. Actual penetration, when the woman is sufficiently lubricated, should not be painful. If tampons have been used then there is unlikely even to be the short pain of the breaking of the hymen. Sometimes, though, nerves can cause the muscles to clamp up in the vagina – which, if it lasts for a significant time, is the condition known as *vaginismus* – and in minor cases is usually overcome by taking time and relaxing. A man needs to learn to take things slowly and lovingly – and realise that the longer he spends on foreplay, the more likely his partner is to enjoy the experience.

Clinical experience shows that in one-night stands, or even short term relationships, men can often have problems both of arousal and performance, too. If this happens, the woman needs to be sensitive, uncritical and take her time arousing him. She can try masturbating him gently until he has a firm erection. Using her mouth on his penis is nearly always arousing or re-arousing, for a man – and it may result in a satisfying experience for her too. If, however, everything fails, don't let it be an issue and try again another day. And this does not mean that she should not be satisfied; he or she can masturbate her to orgasm and let him know that being close to him turns her on.

For a man to climax too quickly, on the other hand, can also leave the woman feeling disappointed and let down. *Premature ejaculation* is particularly common in young and inexperienced men and often occurs the first time they have sex. If this happens, don't panic and see the whole thing as a disaster. The good news is if you stay calm and carry on, the man is much more likely to take longer to orgasm the second time around. Don't rush to try again immediately, though, as men need time (often 10 to 20 minutes) after orgasm before they can be re-aroused. Young men who know that they have a tendency to come sooner than they or their partners would like, could try masturbating before they have a night with their girlfriends to take the edge off their orgasmic urgency.

Wrong time, wrong place

Sex, the first time, often happens where neither partner can relax properly. This is especially true of young couples who perhaps still live with their parents and don't either have sufficient privacy in their own rooms or don't wish to have sex when their parents are around. Making love in the back of a car, or any other semi-public place, can make sex a hurried and sometimes unsatisfying experience – although of course "quickies" can have their own erotic appeal.

Try to find a place and a time when you will not be disturbed, for instance when parents are on holiday, or when you know that they will be out for a certain time. In the latter case, accept the fact that you will not be able to fall asleep in each other's arms afterwards, and stay aware of time. Having to get dressed in a hurry as someone is at the door can put a real dampener on the whole event.

Make sure you have condoms and try to take time in all you do so that you can fully relax in each other's company.

Virgins should tell

If either of you is a virgin, it is best to say so. For a woman, it means that it may hurt if her partner thrusts too deeply too soon, or too fast, so he will have to take care. Unless the vagina is fully lubricated – which only happens when the woman is properly aroused – sex can be painful for both. If the woman is a virgin, the man should probably be on top. Something as simple as placing a pillow under her hips will help make penetration easier, and more comfortable.

Although a man will probably have an erection within seconds and quickly feel the desire to penetrate, a woman will need at least some minutes of foreplay and stimulation before she is ready to receive him. This should be long enough to make sure she is well lubricated, but it may be necessary to provide more. Several lubricants are available from chemists, although saliva is natural, readily available, warm and just as good. In addition, some lubricants – and gels such as vaseline – can cause condoms to split, so check before using.

A man-on-top position can work well for the first time as this makes penetration easier and is more comfortable for the woman. A pillow placed under her hips makes the angle of penetration less acute and is potentially less painful. If the woman is not well lubricated, use saliva or a lubricant that you can buy from a chemist. The man should be guided by her, enter gently, and try not to thrust too deeply or too hard, too soon.

The man should penetrate in a gentle but firm way and make only light, shallow thrusts. It is better for the woman to guide his penis into her vagina with her hands and let him penetrate by pushing against him. In this way she can dictate the speed and depth of penetration.

This will also help the man who is a virgin and who may be worried about how to penetrate for the first time. It will demonstrate to him that she really wants to have him inside her, and how to go about it successfully.

Use a condom

With the rise of sexually transmitted infections, including *AIDS*, it is vital that the man uses a condom. It is always sensible not to take risks with a partner unless you know their sexual history. The fear of having contracted an infection, or equally a fear of pregnancy, can leave either one or both partners desperate with worry and destroy any enjoyment.

Surveys show that the number of unwanted pregnancies from first-time sex is remarkably high.

If you have had unprotected sex or a condom breaks, you can resort to the "morning after pill" available at some pharmacies and walk-in medical centres. If taken within 72 hours, these are usually effective in preventing pregnancy. They do not, though, offer any protection against sexually transmitted infections (STIs).

You must be frank with each other.

Helping each other

Your expectations and excitement will probably be mixed with some apprehension and nervousness - this is completely natural. Try to make your partner feel comfortable. Wear loose-fitting clothes that can be undone easily: fumbling at too many buttons or catches can make anyone feel clumsy and slightly inadequate. Remember also personal hygiene. Many lovers are worried about how their partner will react to their body odours, so bathing or showering beforehand can put your mind at rest, and shows how much you care about your partner.

Orgasm or not

While men rarely experience difficulty in reaching orgasm any time, when women have sex for the first time with a new partner, they can often find it hard to climax. If it is the first time for both of you, the man is likely to climax quickly, which may not give the woman enough time to reach the level of arousal necessary for her to achieve her orgasm. This is all too common with first encounters, and not necessarily a failure. Good lovers learn to take time. As the American sex researcher, Alfred Kinsey, demonstrated, over 90% of women will achieve their orgasm when 20 minutes or more are spent on foreplay. Remember, for the best sex, "the lady comes first", often even before penetration, is a very good rule of thumb for the caring male lover to observe.

DIFFERENT SEX POSITIONS

Man on top

Having Ray on top may seem boring but it means that when he's making love to me, he can talk to me, or suck my breasts, which always turns me on – and also, I can see his face when he climaxes, We have tried lots of different positions, but we always end up like this, as it's the way he likes it best, and I like to feel his body pressing down on me.

Justine

Real lovemaking between two people in a long term relationship has so many aspects to it – all deeply valuable – that the number of positions available in our sexual repertoire can become irrelevant. Many people make love in only one to three positions for their whole time together. It has been said that a good relationship can sustain an indifferent sex life, but that a good sex life will never maintain a poor relationship. However, as long as both partners are willing, broadening their sexual horizons can revitalise your sex life, keep things fresh and exciting and add spice to the relationship.

Even if it is just for special occasions, or in order to learn what we do not want, it is well worth exploring many of the available variations and have lots of loving fun trying them out...

The missionary

Most couples prefer the so-called "missionary" position, for all sorts of physical and emotional reasons. The basic configuration is one where the woman lies on her back with her legs apart and the man penetrates her as he lies on top of her. All the other man-on-top positions are really a variation on this theme.

Most people consider it to be a romantic position. The face-to-face contact ensures that both partners can watch each other's reactions and preferences, and talk and kiss throughout the whole session. They can kiss each other's neck and shoulders and the man can suck the woman's breasts and nipples as he rises and falls on her. This all helps to create a loving atmosphere, and many say that it makes sex more meaningful. For this reason, it is a good position for any couple having sex together for the first time.

It is also a receptive position for the woman. She can relax, and satisfy any desire she may have to relinquish control or even to be dominated during lovemaking, if that is what she likes. For the man, it gives him the majority of control – over rhythm, speed and vigour.

If the woman lies in the missionary position with her legs straight out and the man's legs on top of hers, penetration is not very deep, but the fit is tight and sensations for both are very pleasant. If the man puts his legs outside his partner's legs and uses his thighs to squeeze hers together, he can increase the hold on his penis and make long powerful thrusts. The woman can use her pelvic muscles to grip his penis, as if to milk him as he enters and withdraws, providing him with wonderful sensations and probably making him climax very quickly.

It is worth experimenting with many different leg positions to experience new pleasures. For example, the further back a woman pulls her knees, the deeper penetration becomes. Try wrapping your legs around the man's back, and changing the tilt of your pelvis to increase genital contact. You can also control his thrusts by pulling him towards you or pushing him away in the rhythm you choose.

For the man who has difficulty in maintaining erections, and for the one who climaxes too soon, it is an ideal position for controlling the degree of stimulation his penis receives.

Most times we make love we try all kinds of different positions but always seem to end up with Andy on top. It can make me feel that I'm not wholly doing my bit, you know, just lying there. It doesn't allow me to be as active as I'd like.

Ella

In the missionary position, if the woman raises her knees, it allows for a greater range of movements for the man and deeper penetration. A couple can keep full body contact and kiss and talk to each other all the time.

Deeper penetration

Most men like to penetrate a woman as deeply as possible when they make love, and many women enjoy the sensation of being 'filled up'.

The deepest penetration can be achieved if the woman draws her knees up to her chest and places her legs over the man's shoulders. The man should take his weight on his hands and rock forward to push his penis up against the back wall of her vagina. If he is strong enough, he may be able to hold his weight on one arm for a while, leaving the other hand free to caress her breasts and nipples and even her clitoris. During that time, the woman's hands are free to caress her partner's back, buttocks and anus and, should she wish, she can help achieve her orgasm by stimulating her clitoris.

Try subtle variations on this theme. One leg over the man's shoulders and one under his arm can alter the angle of penetration quite considerably - it stimulates only one side of the vagina, and produces new sensations for you both. But the man must be careful, because if he thrusts too hard and deep he could hit up against one of the ovaries, and this can be painful for some women.

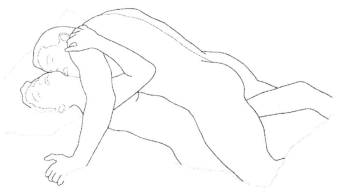

When the man places his legs outside the woman's her thighs provide a firmer grip on his penis and allows for longer, deeper thrusting. It is a good position for the man who needs a lot of penile stimulation to climax.

If the woman tilts her hips and puts both legs over the man's shoulders,
penetration is deepest. This position can be tiring for the man as he
needs to take most of his weight on his hands.

Raising her hips

Raising the woman's hips from the bed can also allow deeper
penetration and powerful sensations. Cup your hands under
her buttocks and lift her up as you kneel between her thighs.
Although this allows your partner virtually no movement, your
thrusts can be deep and can help her reach a high state of

arousal. However the man is supporting most of his partner's weight – so two pillows supporting her hips can be useful.

If the woman is fit and supple enough, she could try arching her back and supporting her weight on her shoulders and feet while the man kneels and enters her from a vertical position rather than from above. An alternative, less tiring way of achieving the same position is for her to sit on the edge of the bed, sofa or a chair and he kneels to enter her.

With all the man-on-top positions, small variations can produce new pleasures for both of you.

By kneeling between the woman's legs as she sits on the edge of the bed,
the man has a considerable range of movements. Simply by swaying his hips,
he can make long or short thrusts in any rhythm

A variation is for the woman to place one leg over the man's shoulder. This allows him to direct his penis to different parts of the vagina, creating new sensations for both.

I like being on top as it is the only way that I feel in control of what we're doing. I like it best if she climaxes first. Just being able to see her body and face makes it much better for me as I can see how excited she is getting and that makes me excited too. I also know when to slow down to help her along.

Charlie

Woman on top

My sexual relationship with Mary hadn't been going that long and I used to go on top most of the time. Perhaps I felt that I always had to be in charge. Then, one time, we'd had a few drinks and, first of all, she stripped for me and then took off my clothes in the slowest most seductive way I could imagine. I just let it happen. The next thing, I was on my back and she was on top of me, kissing me all over, sucking my nipples and treating my penis as if it was the best lollipop she'd ever tasted. For a second I thought, "But I'm the man, I'm supposed to be in control." Then she was putting me inside her and pressing her clitoris onto my stomach. It felt so good not to be having to set the pace, now we just share who's on top – varying it even in the same session. We keep the lights on and it really gets me going to see her moving up and down on me. I can even get a charge from seeing her moistness on my penis.

Michael

This range of positions gives the woman more opportunities to take charge of lovemaking. Men can often feel that they always have to be the ones to initiate sex and be in control, so many of them are turned on by this change around. Before the penis enters the vagina, it can be fun for both partners if the woman teases a little. She can hold her partner's penis firmly, masturbating him while touching her vagina with the tip of it. She can use it to stimulate her clitoris and her vaginal lips. You can play this game until neither of you can, or want to, hold back any longer.

Controlling penetration

Once the penis enters the vagina, the woman can control its angle and the rhythm, depth and speed of the thrusting. She can push or rock backwards and forwards and from side to side, swivelling her pelvis, or moving up and down the shaft of the penis. She can crouch forward to kiss her lover, sit up while he caresses her breasts, reach round to massage his scrotum or anus or lean back to let his penis stimulate her G-spot on the front wall of her vagina.

The man may find that the extent of pelvic movement is restricted the further back the woman leans. This can be an advantage, however: by slowing down, both of you can experiment with the different sensations you can create for each other. The man can twitch his penis inside his lover's vagina, and she can alternately squeeze and relax her vaginal muscles.

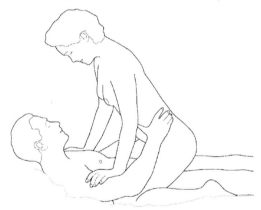

(1) When on top, the woman is free to alter the angle of her body to create exciting sensations for both herself and her partner. She can control the speed and depth of penetration of his penis and direct it to almost any part of her vagina. Sitting upright, she is free to move up and down and rock from side to side, while her partner can help modify her movements by holding her waist, if he enjoys a particular sensation.

(2) If the man sits up, movement may be restricted to a bump and grind motion, but it allows him to kiss her breasts and caress her back and buttocks.

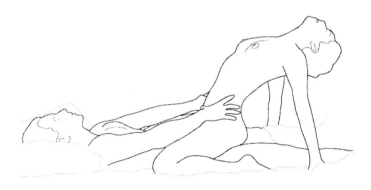

(3) The woman lying back takes her weight off the man's pelvis; and by resting her weight on her knees and arms she is free to control penetration. This variation also allows the man easy access to stimulate her clitoris with his hands.

Stimulating the clitoris

Either squatting or lying, legs back, on top of her partner and simply moving her pelvis backwards and forwards, the woman can stimulate her clitoris by rubbing it against his pubic bone or either can stimulate it.

She can change the angle of her body so the penis touches and stimulates different parts of the vaginal walls. She can also vary the depth of the penis, from its stroking the outer lips, to half way in to touch her G-spot, to full depth where it can massage the cervix at the top of the vagina.

If squatting, she can also reach down and gently tug back the skin of the penis to expose the glans, and then move up and down on it to give him maximum pleasure. This will inevitably make him climax more quickly, but she may not find it as stimulating, as the penis will not penetrate so deeply.

For greater enjoyment for him, she can try strumming the base of his penis with her fingers, just above where it disappears into the man's pubis. While still allowing deep penetration, this also produces exquisite feelings for him. And you may find that you can combine this with stimulating your clitoris.

Woman-on-top positions are also good for practising the squeeze technique, described in Chapter Four. This can help the man control the time it takes for him to have an orgasm, and it is used in the treatment of men with premature ejaculation problems. The basic idea is that you squeeze the end of the penis firmly with your fingers until the man begins to lose his erection. You can then arouse him again and continue making love. If the man feels himself about to climax too soon, he can signal to his partner to squeeze again.

Facing away from the man can be equally exciting. Indeed, swiveling 180 degrees while still on the penis is a whole new pleasure in itself. When the woman is facing away from him, he can massage her buttocks and caress her anus. Many men find it erotic to watch their penis enter the woman in this position. Although you will not be able to look into each other's face, it is a good position for deep penetration, and also for stimulating the front wall of the vagina where the G-spot is located.

To reach the position where the woman is facing away from the man, try swiveling 180 degrees from a face-to-face position while keeping the penis inside the vagina all the time.

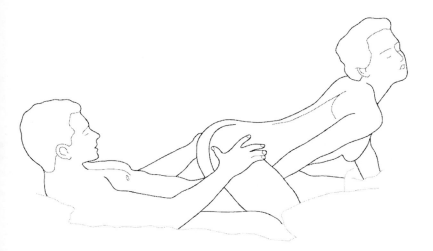

When the woman leans forward, the man can easily see his penis entering the vagina – something many men find highly erotic. This position also gives a clear view of the woman's anus for the man who fantasises about anal sex.

Maybe I'm strange – but when John was on top he would often get the rhythm wrong just at the crucial moment. Just as the first ripples of orgasm were beginning, they'd recede and often they just never came back. That all changed when I got on top. It's now my favourite position. I don't know if it's because I'm more in control or the way we rub against each other, but now I get so wet, and my climax is more in my control when I'm on top.

Ali

Variations

In either of the basic woman-on-top positions – woman facing man, woman facing away – there are delicious variations. The woman can sit with her legs out straight, knees bent, or rest, squatting, on the soles of her feet. While face-to-face, she can rest her legs on his legs. She can also sit sideways on the penis and bring her partner's leg up to her chest; this is a good position for couples who love deep penetration.

There are other comfortable and unusual positions to try. If the man lies on his back and draws his knees up to his chest, the woman can sit halfway along his thighs facing away. It is easier for the woman to direct her partner's penis into her vagina. For the man there is little scope for movement, but the woman can move up and down, sideways and swivel around. Both her hands are free to stimulate her clitoris, and she is always comfortable as she is supported by the man's thighs and the balls of her feet. The penis is at a very acute angle and rubs up against the back wall of the vagina.

The X position

This position is one of the best for female control: the woman lies completely face down, legs astride the man's torso. She can dictate the rhythm, but she can also exercise her vaginal and pelvic floor muscles and hold the penis. It is wonderful for slow intercourse, keeping his orgasm at bay while giving her all the stimulation she needs.

Try to watch and respond to your partner's reactions – facial expressions, breathing – and to massage him or her with a light, or sometimes heavy, touch. This will let you know when your partner is experiencing pleasure, and you can adjust what you do to increase it.

Rear Entry

I find that when we start making love, it is really exciting if he takes me from behind just for a few minutes. It makes me have all kinds of sexy thoughts that get me going. I don't think I often reach orgasm like that, but sometimes when I feel really turned on, just the fact that he pushes into me so deeply makes me feel like I am giving myself to him totally, and I feel relaxed but high at the same time. And the fact that I am totally abandoned seems to excite him too.

Deborah

Positions where the vagina is penetrated from behind are viewed by some as perhaps less romantic than frontal positions, but for both men and women they can be extraordinarily satisfying, and different, especially for couples who have frequent sex.

Because they can be tiring, they may be used as a short interlude during long, passionate sessions. Intense sensations can be felt by both partners, as both are able to move a lot. Penetration can be very deep indeed.

The man is free to caress his partner's breasts and buttocks and can easily reach her clitoris. An added attraction for many men is that they can see their partner's anus, perhaps fantasise about anal sex, and can watch their penis going in and out of her vagina. Many men can also satisfy a need to take charge during lovemaking, and they can thrust very deeply when they ejaculate.

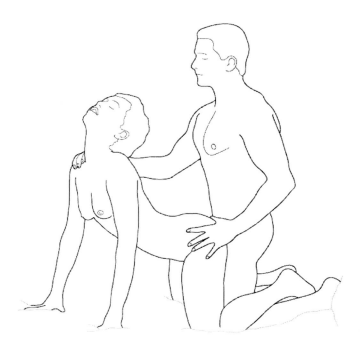

The doggie position - on all fours - allows for very deep penetration. This can be a little painful for some women, which is fine if she is okay with it, but the man should be wholly sensitive to her feelings. He should also bear in mind that rear-entry positions can make a woman feel vulnerable, and be alert to see if he is causing too much discomfort or distress. As a variation, try using the bed as a prop. If the woman kneels with her legs apart at the edge, her hips raised and her weight on her chest and arms, the man can stand behind her and enter. He is free to move as much as he likes by swaying backwards and forwards, and can alter the angle at which the penis enters as he thrusts.

It's really a mixture of things. Feeling him deep inside me is thrilling but just the thought of him looking at my bottom is exciting, too. I'm not in control at all, and the feeling of being taken over like this makes me think quite extraordinary thoughts.

Eliza

Finding the famous G-spot

For a woman, because she cannot see her partner's face, a rear-entry position is ideal for her to stimulate herself whilst indulging her own sexual fantasies. For a woman with a sensitive G-spot, all these positions direct the man's penis on to the front wall of the vagina and can help her achieve the most exquisite orgasms. Even women who do not respond to G-spot stimulation can find themselves enjoying the different sensations.

The most popular rear-entry position is often called the doggie position. The woman kneels down, and then takes her weight on her hands as her partner kneels behind her. The man now guides his penis into the vagina with his hands, although it is often easier if the woman does this herself. Always make sure she is fully aroused and lubricated, as these positions can involve a lot of friction and both of you can become sore quite quickly.

Once the man's penis is inside, take turns to vary the movements. He can lean forward to caress his partner's breasts and clitoris as he moves his penis in and out. Or he can kneel upright and hold his partner's hips, and draw her onto his penis and move her body at a speed and rhythm he enjoys. She can angle her hips or wiggle her bottom in different directions, including pushing on to him, to produce different sensations.

If the woman sways backwards and forwards on the man's penis, that too can be enjoyable.

A variation that allows for very deep penetration is for the woman to rest her chest on the bed as she kneels. If she gets tired she can easily slip down onto her stomach, but then the man will need to take his weight on his hands. In this position there is good friction of his penis, and indirect stimulation of the clitoris and inner lips.

Another possibility is the lateral entry position. Although not well known, it is very restful position for both partners and well worth trying. Also it is one of the very best for the woman who is learning to have orgasms during intercourse. She lies on her back with her legs drawn up, and the man lies at right angles to her and inserts his penis.

Both partners can caress her clitoris and her breasts, and she can reach down to stroke him. Changing the angle of the woman's hips can create different sensations and she can use her legs as levers to push hard back against his thrusts.

And from here, it is worth trying to manoeuvre into a rear-entry position.

When I move into her from behind, it feels totally different from any other position, and just as satisfying for me. I feel I abandon myself much more: a combination of animal lust and the knowledge that she is giving herself to me completely. And the feeling that we are both being much more lustful, if you like, makes us that much closer afterwards.

Andrew

Side by side

Sometimes our lovemaking goes on and on and on. We often try lots of different positions, and tease each other and totally enjoy the feel of our bodies together. But let's face it, some positions are a bit tiring, especially if you carry on for a long time, and your genitals can take a bit of a bashing after a while. We seem to know instinctively if either of us is getting tired, and then usually try the spoons: he can play with my clitoris and we often climax together like this. And then there is that delicious feeling as we drift into sleep – one of his hands on my tummy, the other on my breast and his lips against by neck. It all feels so completely loving and, well, I guess I feel protected as well.

Kate

Romantic, restful and satisfying, side-by-side positions can be just the thing to end a long session of lovemaking or on their own for relaxed, cuddly sex. Facing each other, or nestling like a pair of spoons, these positions allow complete body sensations. There is full body contact, freedom for the hands to reach most of one another's bodies, and faces are close together so a couple can talk and kiss. Adjustments to the two basic positions can allow full and deep penetration, but may restrict the man's thrusting movements. For the couple who want long, leisurely sex, they are ideal.

Face to face

The root of the man's penis can fit tightly against the pubic region when a couple have sex face to face, so the clitoris can receive direct stimulation. Another advantage is that the man's inability to move very much can slow down his orgasmic response. To achieve a face-to-face position, it is quite easy for any couple to roll onto their sides from any of the man-on-top positions. If both partners straighten their legs they can have the delicious sensation of full length body contact and slowly push their pubic areas together. Their arms are free to caress one another's back, face and head. Try grasping one another's buttocks and pulling close together in a steady rhythm.

As with most other positions, slight variations can create vastly different sensations. If the woman slips her legs around the man's waist, his penetration can be deeper and his movements freer. She could try using her feet to massage his buttocks and pull him further into her in time with his thrusting rhythm. At this point, both partners can reach her clitoris with their hands to stimulate it, if they want.

Face to face or spoon positions can be the perfect ones in which to fall asleep together after making love, totally relaxed, with neither partner carrying the weight of the other, close in an intimate embrace.

Front to back

To achieve the classic spoons position, a couple can roll over from a rear-entry position. Otherwise, the woman will need to raise her knees while she is lying on her side, and the man penetrate from below and behind. Penetration is fairly full and the penis can be held quite tightly by the vagina. Variations could be for the man to rub his upper leg over and against his partner's thigh, and draw it softly backwards and forwards to produce gently rocking movements. If the woman now rolls slightly on to her back, the man can place one leg between hers, rub his knee against her stomach, and press firmly on her pubic area for even more intimate stimulation.

This position has tremendous potential for the man to be extremely loving.
His hands are free to caress her breasts and clitoris, and in fact nearly all of her body.
He can kiss and nuzzle the back of her neck and shoulders or reach round to kiss her face
and lips. Some women find this the most intimate of all positions.

Just slowly, gently making love to Catherine while I feel her body completely against mine gives me such deep feelings for her that I wish it could go on forever.

Jake

SPONTANEOUS SEX

Jane and I were walking around the garden at my cousin's wedding when all of a sudden she took my hand and dragged me into the garden shed. She didn't say anything. She just kissed me passionately and started undoing my trousers. Then she leant against one of the walls, unzipped me and guided me in. I started thrusting really hard, and when I thought someone was walking down the garden path, I did it even faster. Suddenly, we both had this explosive orgasm and that was that. Then we walked casually back to the house as if nothing had happened.

Stuart

Instant sex is not just an explosion of passion with no role
in an intimate relationship. Its urgency can reinforce a bond
of trust between any loving couple.

Although intimacy and caring are the foundation for the best and most satisfying sexual relationships, there is still room for spontaneous passion and even, on occasion, instantly satisfying pure lust. Instant sex, when orgasm for either or both partners occurs almost at once, can be extraordinarily exciting. The knowledge that your partner simply cannot wait is, for many people, a huge turn on.

Though a woman will usually need a certain amount of foreplay for her vagina to be fully lubricated and to be receptive to the man's penis, if she is in the mood for passionate sex this can happen almost immediately. If not, there is always nature's own lubricant, saliva. And a man's erection can be almost instantaneous if given the right stimulus: a glimpse of his partner's breasts or buttocks, perhaps under a dressing gown as she walks through the house, can be enough. Very few men are not aroused by a woman who suddenly lifts her skirt and quickly removes her knickers. Likewise, women can be turned on by the sight of a man, often in the most unlikely situations.

Instant sex, or 'quickies', excite because passions run very high and there is not even time to properly remove your clothes. Because your movements are so frenetic they create sensations not experienced at any other time.

In the best of the instant sex positions, neither of you needs to remove any clothes at all. The man can simply release his penis through his trousers while the woman pushes aside the crotch of her knickers. For a man, if she partly releases her breasts – or even just one breast – from a bra or camisole, it can be terrifically exciting. A woman can vastly increase her own excitement by ripping open her partner's shirt, for instance.

There are few boundaries to when and where couples have quickies. For many people, sex in semi-public places, or in a room next to another full of people, adds greatly to the excitement: fear of discovery can be a powerful aphrodisiac. Be careful, though, particularly with al fresco sex not to break any laws of public decency.

We'd spent the afternoon in the garden, when I went in to get some food ready. After about five minutes, Len came into the kitchen. He came up behind me silently, and dropped his jeans, pulled aside my knickers and all I could feel was his hard penis pushing against my bottom. I didn't say anything either, but opened my legs and put my hand down and guided his penis into me. He went into me deeply and hard and I just let go. I loved knowing he wanted me and, well, it was something new that made me feel special.

Hazel

MAKING LOVE

CREATIVE SEX

We do tend to stick to the same routine most of the time, but every now and again we really go for it - real swinging off the chandeliers stuff. Doing these extraordinary things together seems so outrageous that I don't think you could do them with someone you didn't really trust. It happens when we're both feeling especially sexy, or when we've taken extra long over foreplay, so that we're both so worked up that we just want to share those extra sensations that you get in all these sorts of positions.

Sarah

Most couples find their favourite positions they like best over a period of time, and tend to stick to them. Although there is little to recommend sexually athletic positions for their own sake, they can add new excitement to an unexciting sex life and spice to any relationship. For a man, they can rekindle an interest in sex and revive a diminishing sex drive. For a woman, some of the unusual positions can stimulate parts of her body that others cannot.

The more advanced positions do, however, require a certain amount of fitness and suppleness, so be careful, as pulled muscles don't increase sexual pleasure...

The following pages illustrate several advanced positions for you to try, when and if you please, and each one produces different and unique sensations.

The man lies on his back and pulls his legs right back to his chest. The woman now pulls his penis out and down between his legs. With her back to the man she sits on his penis. Not much movement is possible but she can contract her pelvic muscles to squeeze his penis, bounce a little and wriggle from side to side. She can lean backwards between the man's legs to alter the angle of penetration, or forwards, when the man can place his feet on her back. Be careful - this position can be tiring for the man, and an erect penis at such a downward angle can even be painful for some.

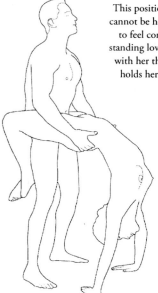

This position requires a strong man and a supple woman, and cannot be held for too long. It does, however, allow the woman to feel completely abandoned. It can be approached from a standing lovemaking position: the woman grips the man's waist with her thighs and puts her arms around his neck. The man holds her by the waist, so she can lower herself backwards.

A more exciting alternative is for the woman to do a handstand in front of the man, who catches her ankles on his shoulders. He should now support her by holding her waist as she opens her legs and brings them down to be opposite his penis. The vulva is fully displayed and he can enter, controlling the rhythm by pushing and pulling the woman's body to and fro. This is the only position that allows entry to be achieved in this way, and provides a unique experience. If the man is strong enough to take the woman's weight with one arm, he can use his other hand to stimulate her clitoris.

MAKING LOVE

Kneeling, with the woman on top, gives good stimulation of both partners' genitals, especially direct stimulation of the clitoris and vaginal lips. This position can be reached from a standard woman-on-top position, or by the man kneeling, or squatting and the woman sliding along his thighs until he can penetrate. It is a position that allows full body contact, and subtle variations can be achieved by either the man or the woman leaning backwards.

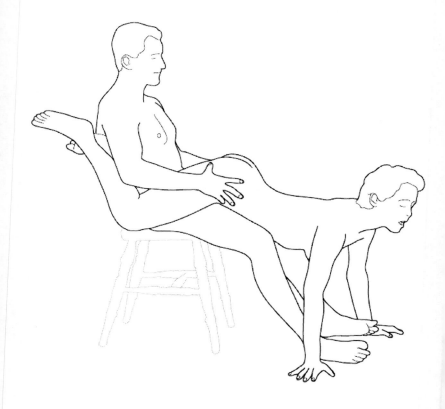

In this position, the man sits on a chair and the woman kneels doggie fashion in front of him. He gently lifts her up and towards him, and she wraps her legs around his waist as he guides his penis inside. The man's movements are restricted, but he controls the woman's movements with his hands on her buttocks. For men who are excited by the sight of their partner's buttocks and anus, it is highly visually stimulating.

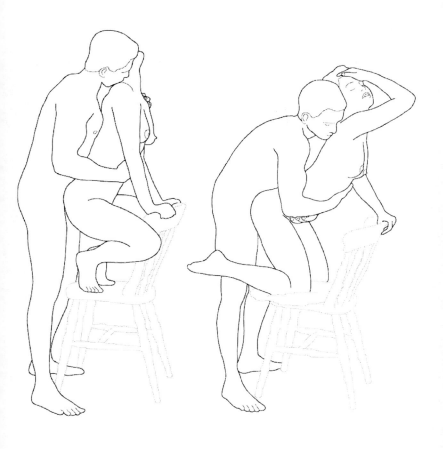

The woman begins by squatting or kneeling on a chair facing away from the man, with hands holding onto the back. He can now enter her from the rear and begin thrusting. For the woman, she enjoys unusual sensations as she feels her partner's penis entering her almost from underneath her. Be careful not to over balance, especially in the rush of orgasm. This position is good for stimulating the G-spot as the penis is directed against the front wall of the vagina. The man is free to kiss his partner's neck and shoulders, caress her breasts and both are free to stimulate her clitoris.

APRES SEX

After he has climaxed, I know that he will shut his eyes and drift off to sleep. I try not to mind, but sometimes I really need a cuddle. So I like it if he stays inside me for as long as possible, even when his penis has gone down. Other times I just snuggle up close, with one of his arms around me, even if he has gone to sleep.

Sophie

In the rounding off a session of satisfying sex, it can be useful for both partners to understand exactly what happens to men and women after orgasm, emotionally and physically. There are differences, and they can lead to misunderstandings that can leave either partner hurt or resentful.

For a woman, resolution from orgasm can be slow as she drifts her focus back into the world. She likes – and, some would even say, needs – to feel her partner embracing her, and enjoys loving kisses and words to make truly intimate lovemaking end warmly.

For a man, however, his erection goes quickly after ejaculation, his penis may feel very sensitive and his sexual feelings desert him. This, with the tiredness that comes with orgasm, makes many men want simply to withdraw, roll over and go to sleep.

Keep talking

In bedrooms all over the world this is what happens night after night, leaving most men ignorant of the damaging emotional effect this can be having on their partner. She can feel neglected, unloved and lonely, especially if she is left unsatisfied. The whole relationship, emotionally and sexually, can very soon begin to suffer.

A sensitive man should try to be tender, and talk to and cuddle his partner even if he feels this overriding need to sleep. It is also up to the woman to keep her lover interested and awake by touch and conversation.

Try making love at other times of the day occasionally, so that neither of you is tired; you will have more energy to cuddle and talk. Avoid talking about mundane things such as shopping or problems with the car; concentrate on each other, the experience you have just had, and how much you enjoyed it.

QUESTION TIME

Q. Are there any good positions for getting pregnant?

A. As a sperm has to pass through the cervix into the womb to fertilise an ovum, positions that allow the semen to be deposited close to the cervix, and to stay there for some time, may help in conception.

Choose a man-on-top position, with the woman's hips slightly raised. These positions allow for deep penetration, and if the woman lies still after her lover has ejaculated, the neck of the womb, the cervix, can remain bathed in his semen. However, if you have been trying to get pregnant for some time without success, it is best to consult your doctor.

Q. When my boyfriend makes love to me from behind I have orgasms that are deeper and much more powerful and deep than in any other position. Why should this be?

A. A rear-entry position directs the penis onto the front wall of the vagina and will stimulate the G-Spot area when the woman is sensitive to it. The orgasms originating from G-Spot stimulation are reputed to be different from those that originate from clitoral stimulation alone. Some women claim that they last longer and are more powerful.

Q. When my partner has a strong orgasm her vagina really seems to flood with liquid. She says she is not urinating but I don't know what's going on.

A. About 10% of all women release fluid from their urethra at orgasm. Female ejaculation is thought to originate from glands that run alongside the urethra and may well be a female equivalent (known as Skein's Glands) of the male prostate. The ejaculate has been shown not to be urine, nor is it increased moisture being secreted from the vaginal walls. It is perfectly normal.

Q. *When my wife is on top I have real difficulty in climaxing, although she seems to be able to climax easily. Is there anything wrong?*

A. The ejaculatory reflex is slowed down when a man lies on his back, making it more difficult for him to climax. Also his range of movements is restricted, so he cannot get the intensity of stimulation he needs. Your partner is in control, so talk to her and show her what you would like and how you need to be stimulated – though you should also be very pleased that she has such a reliable path to achieving her orgasm.

Q. *My husband is always wanting to try all kinds of complicated lovemaking positions, but I don't see the point. Is there really anything to recommend them?*

Athletic and body-bending positions do not need to undertaken for their own sake. Many of the more advanced positions do, however, create unique and very different sensations for both partners. Try them and see if you like them. They can liven things up when your sex life and relationship has become routine and a bit lacklustre.

Q. Is it safe to have sex when you are pregnant, and what are the best positions?

A. Unless you have had a miscarriage, and are advised by your doctor not to have sex during the first few months, sex can continue throughout pregnancy. Very deep penetration is best avoided and certain positions are better than others, especially in the last few months when the woman's abdomen has grown and it is uncomfortable for her to take her partner's weight. Rear-entry, side-by-side and woman-on-top positions should all be comfortable and not put too much pressure on the woman's abdomen.

CHAPTER FOUR
THE OTHER SIDE OF SEX

How to recognise, discuss and overcome difficulties together, along with options for safer sex and contraception.

DIFFICULTIES: RECOGNISING AND OVERCOMING THEM

It would be nice to be able to say that our sex life was always a hundred per cent fantastic and seven nights a week. Actually, when you are younger, you have more energy and fewer commitments. On the one hand you may have had more orgasms a week but now we tend to have much longer sessions which can be deeper and more satisfying, especially for my wife. If neither of us feels like sex, there's no pressure. I think that's because we now have a proper relationship and know we love each other.

Chris

In a long term relationship – that may last for 50 or more years – it is hardly surprising that from time to time, sex is not always as frequent, or intense, as in the early days. On the positive side, research shows that most women find that they have fewer orgasmic difficulties as they head into their 30s. So, whilst men peak sexually in their late teens, it is usually decades later for women.

Sex is a highly complex part of our lives: it is influenced by our past, our present and especially our current moods and emotions outside the bedroom. Tiredness, worries about work or money and poor health are all things that can affect performance and satisfaction in lovemaking. Whatever you feel, forget the myth that sex should score 10 out of 10 every time. That is impossible. Work on the assumption that out of every 10 sessions one or two will be mind-blowing, one or two may be a disaster, and the rest simply OK.

When sex goes wrong, it is best to remember to take things gently and not to worry unnecessarily. Worry itself can turn a minor hiccup into a real problem.

If it is just the odd disappointing episode, you could begin by trying some of the more adventurous sexual positions in the previous chapter. If that fails, then counsellors will often suggest abstaining from intercourse for a few days or so to bring back the urge and get things get back to normal. And always be open to talking about things together, rather than letting any resentments build up. One partner's problems outside the bedroom may result in the other feeling hurt and rejected in bed, simply because he or she is not aware of what is going on.

More persistent problems do occur, however, and may need professional help if they are to be overcome. Some may be physical, others emotional; but mind and body are so closely linked that an emotional problem can often manifest itself physically. The first step in remedying any long-standing issues is to try to understand them yourself, and then to share them with your partner.

There is much you can do for yourselves to put things right.

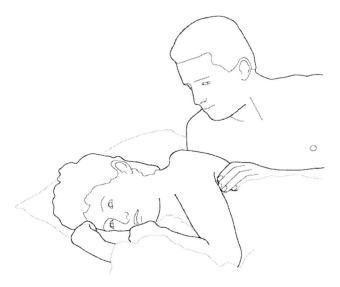

The best form of therapy can be an interested, caring and loving partner.
There is absolutely no point in either blaming the other: most difficulties can
be worked out if you address them together and continue with the intimate
and loving behaviour that is a natural part of a successful relationship.

But if a problem persists, and it is not just a minor hiccup
in your relationship, then it may be worth seeking
professional help.

*I remember we went through an awful period in our sex life a few
years ago. I was really tired from work and didn't want sex. Then I
started to have these painful vaginal spasms which made
intercourse very difficult. It really worried us at first, but Mike was
fantastic. We stopped having intercourse and concentrated on other
things, caressing each other and oral sex. After a month or so, with
all the pressure off, the problem just disappeared.*

Ella

Female sexual difficulties

For men, orgasm is the response to sufficient physical stimulation of an erect penis. Some, though, can have orgasmic difficulties of premature ejaculation or, on the other hand, taking too long, known as *anorgasmia*, and may even fake orgasm. For women, there are all kinds of reasons why they can have orgasm problems and these are rarely wholly physical. Female orgasm is complex, and much more linked to mental and emotional aspects of her life. A woman may find it hard to reach orgasm simply because her mind is elsewhere, she is worried about work, love or money, family or friends. Reasons can range from deep-seated issues from the past to simply being very tired.

All that said, the physical aspect is also extremely important for women and the most common cause for not reaching orgasm is lack of arousal. This can be especially true for young couples. If the man learns and understands his partner's needs, and takes time with foreplay before penetration, it can make a real difference. It has already been noted that over 90% of women are likely to achieve their orgasm when 20 minutes or more is spent on foreplay – and that many good lovers enjoy helping their partners to achieve an orgasm even prior to penetration.

While most women find penetrative intercourse enjoyable, the vast majority do not have an orgasm from penetration alone during lovemaking. Without sufficient stimulation of the clitoris, orgasm is unlikely, so it is important for men to focus on this first. Studies have shown that whilst women can be as quick as men to reach orgasm by masturbation alone (around three to five minutes), in penetrative intercourse alone, the man orgasms as quickly as by manual stimulation, but women can take on average 18 minutes to achieve their orgasm.

Couples should work together to change their lovemaking techniques to include what will make orgasm more likely for the woman. To begin with, this will often need to involve more loving behaviour in everyday life to create a greater feeling of emotional intimacy in general, and then, in particular, much greater time and care on the part of the man during sex itself.

Begin by paying plenty of attention, manually and orally, to the clitoris. Use positions that give maximum stimulation to the clitoris – or a position that allows either partner to stimulate the clitoral region manually during penetration. It is often said, too, though, that good orgasms are more likely to be the outcome of a good relationship than of a good technique.

Vaginismus

Occasionally, painful muscle spasms contract the entrance to the vagina, and this can make intercourse difficult or even physically impossible. Mild attacks can occur, though rarely, even in women who have had pain-free sex for years, but more often in young women. The causes are many, and usually most of them are not serious. Poor arousal, apprehension about making love, guilt, inexperience, or the fear of pain, can all contribute. The man should not coerce the woman or make her feel in any way guilty and he should recognise that this is a reflex action over which the woman has no control.

Self help for this complaint can be quite easy if the problem is a new one; talking about it with a loving partner should help the woman embark on a fulfilling sex life again quite soon. Her problem could be a simple, but very reasonable,   fear of pregnancy, which can be overcome with reliable contraception. However, there may be deeper-seated problems, such as unhappy early sexual experiences.

If the problem is relatively minor for the woman, this simple training programme might help.

When you are feeling relaxed, use a hand mirror and look at your vagina. Then, place a well-lubricated finger at the entrance of the vagina and insert it shallowly. Leave it there for a moment and get used to how it feels. Gradually insert your finger deeper. If you feel your vaginal muscles beginning to tighten, contract the muscles yourself and then relax them. Now you can repeat the cycle: insert one finger deeper, and eventually two fingers, over a period of time. Gradually, you will learn to control your vaginal muscles and relax them.

You may also wish now to involve your partner, allowing him to insert his well-lubricated finger slowly into her vagina until it contracts. At this point he should hold his finger still until you relax again, and always penetrate only as far as you wants. This is usually best done after you have become confident with your own fingers. Always make sure that you control the penetration.

Once you have overcome the anxiety of having something in your vagina, you can progress at whatever rate suits you. You may not want to go for intercourse too soon – only when you feel completely at ease about it. Choose a woman-on-top position at first, so that you can control the depth and speed of penetration.

In the early stages, it is best if the man makes no attempt to thrust.

This programme takes patience, but it can pay dividends. If this kind of DIY therapy does not produce the results you want, then you should seek help from your doctor.

Male sexual difficulties

Men can find that they cannot keep an erection long enough to have sex or are put off their stroke at some point during sex and then climax slips away from them.

Generally, these are one-off occasions and should provide no basis for long-term worry. Too much alcohol, and (just as with women) tiredness and the worries of everyday life, can be the reason. The important thing here is for the man's partner to try and be understanding, never critical, and recognise that putting pressure on the man to perform, in these circumstances, will only make it more difficult for him.

Long-term impotence, however, can create real problems in a relationship. While a woman can still enjoy sex to some degree, even if she has problems with orgasm, a man must have an erection if anything is to happen at all. Though it may be necessary to seek professional advice eventually, there are things that a couple can try for themselves to begin with.

The first is to try to discover the nature of the problem together; the most successful therapy could well be a caring and interested partner. It may be due to medical reasons: a tight foreskin that is painful when the man erects *(phimosis)*, medication prescribed by doctors, illegal drugs such as marijuana, or legal ones such as tobacco and alcohol.

Legal prescription drugs, for instance those for high blood pressure and anti-depressants, can cause impotence and affect libido. Viagra, Cialis, Levitra and drugs like them are available on prescription for erectile dysfunction (when a man finds erection difficult, short-lived or impossible). A word of warning: be careful about trying to save money by buying such drugs on the internet - you may be getting something rather different from what you think you are paying for.

A Viagra pill takes about half an hour to work and can produce an erection, though this will still only happen in response to sexual stimulation – but much more readily. It allows more blood to flow to the sponge-like tissue in the penis, causing it to swell and harden. The stories about constant erections are rarely true (though medical help should be sought if one should persist for more than four hours); when a man is no longer sexually excited, it will usually go away as normal. Viagra is not chemically addictive (though it may bring about a degree of psychological dependence), or an aphrodisiac.

Premature ejaculation

This problem, in which the man climaxes very quickly – sometimes after only a few seconds of his penis being inside the vagina, or even before penetration – is quite common in young men and can be very frustrating for both partners.

Do not despair. It can be one of the easiest problems to deal with, either alone or as a couple.

The man needs to train his ejaculatory reflexes so that he can learn to control them. He should begin by recognising the sensations that signal that he is about to climax, the moments before he reaches the point of no return. Most men learn this naturally during their youth while masturbating.

Then a manoeuvre known as the squeeze technique, used over a period of weeks, can often sort out the problem and a man should soon be able to control his ejaculations.

During masturbation, when he feels that he is about to come, the man should firmly squeeze the end of his penis just under the ridge around the head, at the frenum, with his thumb and two fingers. After about 15 seconds his erection will then usually begin to subside. He can then re-arouse himself and try again. Gradually, he will be able to keep an erection for longer without climaxing.

Now it is time to involve the woman. She should masturbate the man, and when he is just about to reach the point of no return of ejaculation, he should signal this to her. She can now apply the squeeze technique herself. Over a period of time, the man will learn to control his natural urge to climax, even in a highly erotic situation.

The next step is for the man to penetrate his partner. Choose a woman-on-top position (this reduces the man's ejaculatory reflex) and, again, he should say or signal to his partner when he senses that he is about to climax. In this position it is possible for her to quickly slip off his penis, and apply the squeeze technique until he gains control. Lovers should repeat this cycle until the man is confident that he can remain inside the woman without ejaculating for as long as they want.

A programme like this may need to be practiced over several weeks, and may be tedious for the woman. However, the investment of time and love should be well worth it in the long run.

Until your confidence has grown, try positions where the man is less stimulated. Positions that allow deep penetration, such as rear-entry or side-by-side, can also be used; when a woman is highly aroused the end of the vagina balloons at its top end, so there is less friction on the head of the penis. As long as the man controls his thrusting, he will find that there can be less stimulation even when he penetrates deeply.

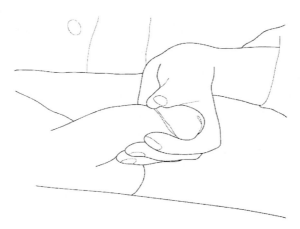

The squeeze technique involves one or other of you grasping the penis just below the head, or glans, before the man ejaculates. Use your fingers and thumb and press firmly for about 15 seconds, until the man's erection has subsided.

THE OTHER SIDE OF SEX

Getting couples back to enjoying sex:
Sensate focusing

If the problem is in the mind, one option is to embark on a self-help therapy known as sensate focusing.

This is a set of techniques used to gradually reawaken sexual feelings in someone who is feeling unresponsive. This therapy consists of three stages, introduced over a period of a few weeks.

The first stage is to explore your own body, massaging and stroking it to rediscover sensual feelings. The aim is to concentrate solely on your feelings at the time, not to worry about sexual intercourse at all.

The second stage is to involve your partner. Take it in turns to massage each other all over and talk about your feelings and what gives you pleasure. At this stage you should agree not to touch each other's genitals or the highly sensitive parts of your bodies.

After a week, or when you feel comfortable, it is time to move on.

The third stage involves touching one another's sexually sensitive, or erogenous, zones and the genitals. Talk to each other all the time. During these sessions one or other of you may be eager for intercourse, but it is essential for the quicker partner to wait until the other catches up. Proceed at your own pace, and only have intercourse when you both feel ready.

CONTRACEPTION

I used to carry a condom around with me just in case, because I knew I should, and liked to think I was responsible. But when I first was about to sleep with Sue, I was too embarrassed to put one on in case it ruined the mood or I didn't do it right. I was really surprised when she just got one out of her bag and put it by the side of the bed. Then when we got really excited she stopped and picked it up. She kept one hand on my penis, masturbating me gently and keeping me hard as she rolled it down over me. It was very exciting and I nearly climaxed right then. Now when we make love we always use one. It's never an issue - just part of our lovemaking.

Andy

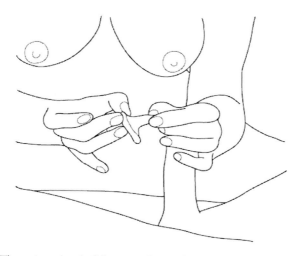

The penis needs to be fully erect to fit a condom on to it properly. When you are both ready for intercourse, keep his erection firm by using your hands, or even your mouth. If the condom is to be fitted by the woman, the man can easily masturbate himself gently to keep a good erection. Make sure the condom is not inside out, squeeze the air out of the teat and then place it over the tip of the penis and roll it down.

Contraception is, like many things in life, a matter of choice; there is a wide range of methods to choose from. But preferences and needs can change as circumstances alter, and, anyway, what is best for one person or couple may not be best for another. Contraception should never be only the woman's responsibility. It is important that both partners discuss the method they want to use. Some are for men only, such as the condom. For women, methods include the diaphragm and the Pill, the cap, the sponge... Try them all to see which suit you best, and do not feel embarrassed to ask questions. Your doctor or clinic will advise you and give you information to read.

Condoms

The great advantage of condoms are that they have very few side-effects or medical risks, and are easily available. They can not only protect you from pregnancy but also from many STIs.

Some couples fear that using condoms may mean that sex loses some of its spontaneity, and that it could ruin the mood to stop in the middle of lovemaking to put one. This doesn't have to be the case; it can be turned into an exciting part of foreplay. Condoms come in all kinds of sizes, colours, textures and thicknesses; using different sorts, and integrating them into your foreplay, can be made fun in itself.

How to use a condom

Unless you are using another form of contraception, and one you trust, you should use a condom every time you have sex to avoid pregnancy, and if you want to make sure you and your partner are safe from the risk of passing on – or receiving – most sexually transmitted infections (STIs).

You should not allow *any contact at all* between the man's penis and the woman's vagina until the condom is on. This is because semen easily leaks from the penis during foreplay, and will almost certainly do so if you have intercourse. It is best therefore to put on a condom when the penis is first erect, not at the last minute, just before the man wants to climax.

When you remove the condom from its foil wrapper, press the air from the closed end before unrolling it slowly down the shaft of the erect penis. Keep stimulating the penis to keep it hard, as a man can lose his erection slightly at this point. When the condom is fully unrolled, make sure that it fits firmly around the base of the penis, and that there is about half a centimetre of space left at the tip if does not have a built-in teat to collect the semen.

During intercourse, it makes sense to check that the condom is still on correctly – a long and energetic lovemaking session can sometimes cause it to ride up, and even slip off.

Once the man has ejaculated, he should withdraw his penis from the vagina before it becomes too limp, otherwise the condom can slide off, allowing the semen to spill out, which defeats the object of using one. One of you can hold the base of the condom tight against the root of the penis to make sure it stays in place as the man withdraws. When the woman takes charge of this, it can be reassuring for her to know that she has some control over the proceedings.

Some couples find that even the very thinnest of sheaths reduces the sensations felt by the penis or the vagina. This may be an advantage for a man who is prone to premature ejaculation but if your lovemaking is less exciting for either of you when you use a condom, and if you are both confident that there is no danger of a sexually transmitted infection, you could try another contraceptive method.

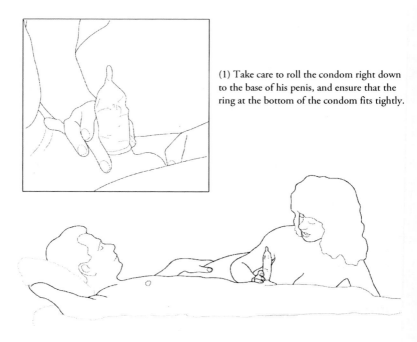

(1) Take care to roll the condom right down to the base of his penis, and ensure that the ring at the bottom of the condom fits tightly.

(2) With practice it soon becomes very easy to fit a sheath quite quickly, so that you need hardly even break the rhythm of your lovemaking.

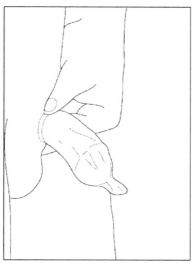

(3) After ejaculation, the man should withdraw before his penis becomes limp, holding on to the base of the condom so that it does not slip off and risk spilling the semen inside the vagina.

THE OTHER SIDE OF SEX

The cap or diaphragm

The cap, or diaphragm, is a rubber dome with a fine metal spring at its rim to keep its shape and keep it in place. The woman inserts it into her vagina and places it across the cervix to act as a barrier against sperm. The cap should always be used in conjunction with a spermicide – available from chemists – spread on both sides and around its rim. After intercourse, leave it in for at least six hours to make sure that all sperm are destroyed or at least immobilised.

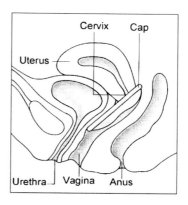

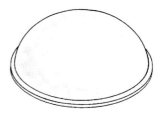

The cap, or diaphragm, has the advantage of having few side-effects and is easy to use.

Some couples find that inserting the cap discourages spontaneous lovemaking, and that spermicides can be messy. The woman can avoid this by inserting the cap some time before an anticipated lovemaking session; but only a maximum of three hours before you plan to have sex. If the wait is longer than this, you should add more spermicide. And if you make love more than once, add more again. Afterwards, wash the cap in warm soapy water, rinse it, dry it and store it in a cool place. Regularly check it for holes or tears.

Diaphragms are available from your doctor or specialist clinic who will help you choose the best kind for you, help you to fit it and show you how to use it. It is essential to have it checked for size every six months, as the shape of your vagina can actually change. Have a new one prescribed each year anyway.

The Pill

The Pill is one of the most effective contraceptive methods, and in the early years of a relationship, so long as both partners are STI free, it is often the favourite because it is easy to use, extremely reliable and allows uninhibited lovemaking.

It has positive and negative side effects, so do discuss these with your doctor to ensure you get the best one for you. The Pill makes a woman's periods shorter, lighter and usually pain free. It can help acne, and research has indicated that it can also reduce your chance of getting cancers of the ovary, womb and bowel.

On the negative side, there are as yet unconfirmed links with breast, liver and cervical cancer, and with heart conditions, especially for longer term users.

Women who smoke, are overweight, diabetic or suffer from high blood pressure are more at risk, and weight fluctuations, headaches and depression must be addressed, possibly just with a change of brand. Those who have severe migraine attacks should be discouraged from taking it.

The Pill works by releasing two hormones, oestrogen and progesterone, similar to the natural ones, produced by the ovaries. The effect is to stop the ovaries from releasing a monthly egg, or ovum, so pregnancy cannot occur. The Pill method usually consists of 21 or 28 daily doses; menstruation occurs after the 28th day.

Another kind of Pill, often called the Mini Pill, relies entirely on progestogen, the general name for the group of hormones including progesterone, for its effect. It does not stop ovulation altogether, but certainly suppresses it, and works in conjunction with the effect it has on the uterus, cervix and Fallopian tubes to make them unreceptive to sperm.

The Pill is usually fine for younger women who do not have any risk factors, but after about 40, there can be a higher risk of having a thrombosis, and thus you should consider switching either to the Mini Pill, or another method of contraception.

The Pill is very useful if you want to delay having a period for a special occasion, such as a holiday. By taking two packets back-to-back without a week's break you can avoid having your period at an inconvenient time.

It is, however, not infallible, and nor are you. Although it can be nearly 100% effective, if you forget one, especially and the beginning or end of a pack, or if you have diarrhea and vomiting (which can happen on holiday as well as at home) its effectiveness is reduced. You should also take extra precautions, such as a condom, if you have been prescribed a course of antibiotics. As always, check with your doctor.

When we first got married I was on the Pill, but then Peter got a posting abroad and I stopped taking it – there seemed little point. Now he uses a condom or I use a diaphragm when Peter's home. Either way's easy and absolutely no problem.

Briony

Morning-after methods

If you are worried that your contraceptive may have failed (a condom has torn, a cap has slipped, or you had sex without contraception) there are two morning-after methods that can be prescribed by your doctor, at some pharmacies or at walk-in clinics. The morning-after Pill can be taken within three days of intercourse and is essentially a strong dose of the contraceptive Pill. A coil, if fitted within five days of intercourse, will usually also bring on the start of menstruation.

But it is important to remember that a woman or a couple should use these methods only in an emergency. It is always best to use some form of reliable contraception every time you have sex.

The coil

The coil, or more correctly the Intra Uterine Device (IUD), is a flat flexible device that is fitted into the uterus, or womb, by a doctor or a trained nurse. It stops embryos implanting in the womb so pregnancy does not occur. It is not 100% reliable, can cause discomfort and does have some significant side-effects for some women, but, after the Pill, IUDs give the next most reliable results. Once inserted, some types of coil can be left in for years to provide trouble-free contraception and uninterrupted lovemaking. Again, you should have regular check ups with your doctor or clinic.

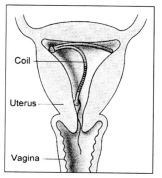
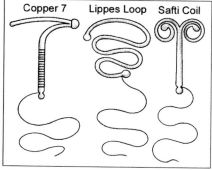

Most makes of the coil provide safe contraception
(though some have caused injury).

The female condom

The newest barrier contraception is the female condom. It is a polyurethane tube, open at one end and closed at the other, that forms a flexible lining when it is inserted into the vagina. Like the male condom, it prevents semen from entering the woman's body, and it also gives good protection against sexually transmitted diseases. A new one *must* be used every time you have intercourse.

Vasectomy and sterilisation

For the couple who have completed their family, these are now the most popular methods of contraception. Vasectomy involves a minor operation to cut the tubes that carry the man's sperm from his testes. Sterilisation involves operating on the woman's Fallopian tubes – they carry the eggs from her ovaries – which can be tied, clipped or cauterised, so that her ova can never meet her partner's sperm.

Make sure you both understand that both of these operations should be considered permanent. If you think you may want children in the future, it is best not to have them; sometimes the procedures can be reversed, but not often.

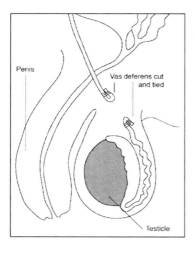

In a vasectomy operation the vas deferens, which carry sperm from each testicle, are cut and tied so that no sperm can reach the penis when the man has an orgasm.

Sterilisation for women involves the cutting and tying of the Fallopian tubes so that ova cannot reach the uterus where they could be fertilised by sperm. Both these methods of contraception should be regarded as permanent.

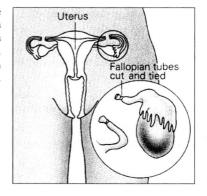

THE OTHER SIDE OF SEX

NATURAL METHODS

Some couples, for health or religious reasons, choose natural family planning. It can be a sophisticated adaptation of the calendar-based rhythm method, identifying a woman's fertile days from changes in her cervical mucus and body temperature.

The calendar method

A woman usually ovulates about two weeks before the start of her next period. As sperm can stay alive inside a woman for five days, and an egg for about two, it means that a couple using this method must abstain from sex for about a week either side of ovulation. But since it is quite common for periods to be irregular, and all kinds of emotional and physical factors can upset the onset of ovulation, the calendar method is now considered unreliable and is no longer widely recommended.

The temperature method

The woman takes her body temperature every morning when she wakes up, and logs it on a special chart. Immediately before ovulation, her body temperature drops slightly, and after ovulation it rises.

Ovulation can also be detected by changes in a woman's cervical mucus. During her fertile period her natural vaginal discharge becomes clearer, less sticky and there is more of it. When it becomes cloudy, sticky and thicker it is safe to have intercourse.

By combining these methods, and using a condom or a cap during fertile days, a couple can have relatively risk-free intercourse all month long. Again, your doctor or clinic will only be too pleased to give advice.

SEXUALLY TRANSMITTED INFECTIONS (STIs)

Well, yes I have had unprotected sex. Somehow at the time it didn't occur to me that I could be killing myself. Maybe it was the excitement – or maybe it was the beer. She also told me she was on the Pill, which somehow made it more difficult for me to insist on wearing a condom. Anyway, everything seemed to be going great, and I suppose I thought if I went out to get a packet of condoms she would have gone off the idea. Well, when I woke up the next day it really hit me and I began to worry a lot. Like, who was she? Who had she been with? It took me about a week to pluck up the courage to go to the clinic. I went, and found I had a mild case of what they called non-specific urethritis. It was cleared up quite quickly with antibiotics - but I am never going to put myself through that again.

Dave

Like any other part of our body, our genitals can be affected by disease, and some of these infections are passed between lovers.

At one end of the scale there are simple infections such as *thrush*, which a woman can acquire spontaneously and not from her partner. These can be irritating and cause frustration, but can be sorted out very quickly. At the other, there are the incurable ones such as the *HIV* virus, which can go on to develop into *AIDS*, which up until very recently was fatal.

Whatever the symptoms, STIs are never trivial and should never be ignored.

If you have the slightest suspicion that you may have been infected, even in a long term relationship, you should abstain from intercourse immediately and make an appointment with your doctor, or a special genito-urinary medicine clinic, whose staff are used to dealing with anxious patients and confidentiality is assured. It is quite common to have more than one infection, and clinics are able to carry out the appropriate tests to make a correct diagnosis, and to prescribe the necessary treatment.

Avoiding STIs

Sex is never completely risk free, and simply the more partners you have, the more at risk you put yourself. It is simply impossible to be sure of anyone's sexual history. One way to prevent STIs, therefore, is to stay faithful to one sexual partner who is faithful to you. Though this, of course, is rarely possible, when most people have several relationships in a sexual lifetime.

There are, however, certain sensible precautions both men and women can take. Always insist on using a condom – over and above any other kind of contraceptive – if you are having sex with someone whose sexual history you are unsure of. It is advisable for both partners to be checked before abandoning the use of condoms.

General hygiene also helps, so wash your genital area and anus daily, and always wear clean underwear. Women should wipe themselves after using the toilet – from front to back so as not to spread bacteria from the anus to the vagina.

If you look under the Health section on *www.loversguide.com* there are full pages on each of the STIs.

Vaginal infections

Thrush, *trichomoniasis* and *bacterial vaginosis* are all infections of the vagina. Thrush is caused by yeasts which may be already present and can occur spontaneously at certain times of life.

The first signs are itching of the vulva and perineum, and a whitish discharge. The skin may become inflamed and scaly, and a rash appear on the inside of the thighs. This can sometimes be passed on to a lover who can have a rash on his penis.

The first thing to do is to refrain from intercourse and get treatment from your doctor, rather than try any homemade cures. Both partners must be completely clear of the infection before resuming lovemaking, or they can play infection pingpong – reinfecting each other back and forth.

Trichomoniasis, or *trich* as it is often called, is another infection of the vagina but can also infect the cervix, bladder and urethra in women, and the urethra and prostate gland in men. As many as 90% of men with infected partners will catch it. In both sexes, it produces a burning sensation when passing urine.

The woman will have an itchy yellow discharge from her vagina, and general soreness. The man may have an occasional discharge from his penis. This disease can be treated by drugs prescribed by your doctor, and it is essential that all sexual partners should be treated too.

Bacterial vaginosis is one of the commonest causes of vaginal discharge nowadays. It produces a smelly discharge, with the odour being most noticeable after intercourse. It is not usually associated with itch, and can be easily treated by your doctor. It can sometimes recur, and if this happens it is wise to treat the male sexual partner too, even though most men have no symptoms.

Urethritis

Nowadays, the most common cause of *urethritis* is *chlamydial* infection. Special tests can identify the cause, and genito-urinary medicine clinics are best placed to carry these out.

The first sign that a woman is infected may be an unpleasant-smelling, yellow discharge. If the infection is left untreated the symptoms may become more obvious. You may suffer from back pain, abdominal pain and fever, experience vaginal soreness or bleeding after making love, or perhaps a stinging sensation when passing urine.

The infection usually resides in the cervix (neck of the womb) from which it can ascend into the Fallopian tubes – through which the ova pass from the ovaries to the uterus – and produce a pelvic inflammatory disease. This can result in pain and even the risk of infertility.

Chlamydia can also be passed on from mother to baby during birth. Infected babies can develop severe conjunctivitis, respiratory infections and pneumonia, and have an increased risk of perinatal mortality (death in the first week of life).

Although *chlamydia* is primarily transmitted through sexual contact it can also be carried into the womb on surgical instruments during any gynaecological procedure which requires the cervix to be opened.

The awkward fact is that because up to 40% of women have no symptoms at all, the first sign that something is wrong may appear in their partner. If he has a discharge from his penis, painful testicles or pain on passing urine, it is vital that you are both tested immediately and treated if necessary.

In men, it has been discovered that *chlamydia* is responsible for around 50% of *non-specific urethritis (NSU)* and can also cause *epididymitis*, an inflammation of the sperm duct and a major cause of male infertility.

Treatment – for both of you – is simple. You will be examined at the clinic by a nurse or doctor, and a sample of mucus will be taken from the cervix and with the man from the urethra. If antibodies to *chlamydia* are found, you have the infection, which can be simply and completely cured with a course of antibiotics.

Until screening becomes more widely available, all sexually active women must look out for symptoms of the disease in themselves and in their partners.

Gonorrhea

This is also a common cause of urethral discharge, although it is not as prevalent as it was in the past. In men, discharges are sometimes more profuse than with *chlamydial* infection. But again, many women with this infection have no symptoms – although both *gonorrhea* and *chlamydia* can produce a yellow vaginal discharge. It is possible to have these infections in the throat, if you practise oral sex. The rectum (back passage) too can be infected, for those practising anal sex, and in the case of some women where the infection spreads across the perineum from the vagina to the anus. Treatment is usually simple, with antibiotics prescribed by your doctor.

Genital ulcers

Genital herpes is a viral infection caused by two closely related viruses: *herpes simplex 1* and *herpes simplex 2*. *Herpes simplex 1* is responsible for about 10 per cent of infections, and is the same virus responsible for cold sores; it can be transmitted from the mouth to the genitals through oral sex.

Once you've got it, it's with you for life. It remains dormant in the nervous system, until you are tired or run down.

The first attack is usually the worst. Within around two to 20 days after exposure to the virus, the skin becomes red, tingly and sensitive. Blisters form on or around the genitals which then rupture to form ulcers. After a few days the blisters burst, and begin to form scabs which may take two weeks to heal.

Flu-like symptoms may also be present, including headaches, fever, muscle ache and swollen lymph-glands. The symptoms may last for several weeks – although in some, the symptoms may be so mild that they go unnoticed.

While there is no cure for *herpes*, some anti-viral drugs are effective in lessening the impact of an outbreak. You might try bathing the infected area in salty water or antiseptics, taking painkillers and wearing comfortable, loose-fitting underclothes.

To avoid transmission, don't have sex during an outbreak. It is highly contagious when it is active, with a 90 per cent chance of being passed on. Even condoms will only offer protection if they fully cover the infected area. It is also possible to transmit the virus during a dormant period, but this is less common.

Many people get depressed, and want to avoid having sex, but try not to let *herpes* get you down. Contact one of the counselling and self-help groups that have been set up to help you cope and realise that you are not alone.

Syphilis is caused by a bacterium which penetrates the skin during sexual intercourse, and produces an ulcer in the genital area, usually within about three weeks, although it can take up to three months for it to appear. It affects both men and women.

Sometimes the ulcer is not particularly noticeable, and in any case it is usually painless. For this reason it may be missed, and only detected when the secondary stage is reached, some weeks later. At that time there may be a rash, fever and swollen glands. However, these symptoms too, may be minimal and go unnoticed.

Proper diagnosis can only be made with a routine blood test in a specialist clinic. It is also carried out on all pregnant women, as the infection can spread to babies in the womb.

The late stages of *syphilis* affects the heart and the nervous system and can be fatal, but because the infection is easily treated with antibiotics, this is extremely rare today.

Genital warts

These are caused by the same virus that causes warts on other parts of the body, but are usually – although not always – contracted from a sexual partner who has them. They appear on the vagina and penis from one to 12 months after sexual contact. They often disappear spontaneously, but your local clinic or doctor can remove them by freezing or other means.

They may re-occur and, as there is a link to cervical cancer in women, it is essential to refrain from intercourse as soon as you see them. Women with *genital warts* should have regular cervical smear tests.

AIDS

Acquired Immunodeficiency Syndrome (AIDS) is caused by a virus, the *Human Immunodeficiency Virus (HIV)*.

Once inside the body, the virus attacks a particular group of blood cells – the T-helper white cells – that play a vital role in defending the body against disease.

The virus invades the T-cells and incorporates itself in the T-cells' genetic material. Here it multiplies and lies dormant.

Eventually the T-cell bursts and *HIV* particles are released into the bloodstream, where they attack more white T-cells.

As T-cells are destroyed, the body's defence system weakens; it becomes susceptible to attack from other diseases such as infections and cancer, from which most *AIDS* patients can eventually die, without medication. Because the virus can lie dormant for so long, many sufferers do not know they are afflicted perhaps for several years after infection.

HIV can be passed on through body fluids, especially blood, semen and vaginal fluid. This means that vaginal, oral and, in particular, anal intercourse with an infected partner can all put you at risk. At present there is no cure for *AIDS* but modern treatments can usually prevent it from being fatal.

It is accepted that the virus cannot pass through latex barriers; therefore condoms at present offer the best form of protection – other than celibacy or complete fidelity.

Tell your partners

Above all, if you are diagnosed with any sexually transmitted infection, tell your partners. It is absolutely essential that all your sexual partners are traced and checked for infection, however difficult it is for you. There is always a chance they will infect someone else.

What you should know to keep your sex life healthy and free of infection

- Condoms help to protect you against sexually transmitted diseases, including the *AIDS* virus, so always wear one with a new partner, or one whose sexual history you are unsure of, even if other forms of contraception are being used. Always use a new one, ensure that it is undamaged, put it on after the penis becomes erect but before contact with a partner's genitals, and hold it firmly when the penis is withdrawn so that no semen is spilled. Dispose of used condoms carefully.

- Oral sex carries risks because there is always a chance that the *HIV* virus could pass from the man's semen into the other person's body

- The fewer sexual partners you have, the less chance you have to come into contact with someone who has an STI or the *HIV* virus

- The fewer partners your partner has, the less risk there is of you getting an STI

- The type of sex you practise affects the risk of catching *AIDS*. Of course, you will only catch *AIDS* if you have sex with an infected partner

- Anal intercourse is particularly risky. This may be because the linings of the anus and rectum are much more delicate than the vagina, making it easier for the virus to pass from one person to another, or because injury is more likely to occur with this form of sex

- Unprotected vaginal intercourse is risky

- Any practice that breaks the skin, or draws blood, either inside the vagina or anus or on the skin, could increase the risk of getting an STI or the *HIV* virus

- Sharing sex toys such as vibrators can be risky, as they could carry the infection from one person to another

- Never share hypodermic needles

QUESTION TIME

Q. Can you get AIDS from oral sex?

A. As with any form of unprotected sex, yes, although there is a lower risk than with vaginal or anal intercourse. Any sexual activity where body fluids come into contact brings the risk of infection, not just from *AIDS* but from a whole range of sexually transmitted diseases.

Q. Although my girlfriend will do virtually anything when we get down to it, she nearly always finds some excuse to avoid full-on sex, or I have to really insist and then it's no good for either of us. What should I do?

A. The first thing to do is to examine your relationship. Was she happy to have sex with previous boyfriends (so is it something about you or this relationship?) or is it that she doesn't want sex generally? Ensure that she is not worried about pregnancy or infections; reassuring her about you using condoms may help her feel more secure about intercourse. There may, of course, be more deep-seated reasons but, if so, she will probably need professional help to overcome these issues.

Q. I find intercourse painful when my husband penetrates me. What should I do?

A. There a several possible reasons why you feel pain. The most obvious is that you are not sufficiently aroused and lubricated. It is therefore up to your husband to spend more time stimulating you until you are aroused enough; and/or try using a lubricant. Opening your legs wide and bending your knees can make penetration easier. It is also possible that you may be suffering from an infection, you may have a case of *vaginismus*, or – though this is rare – there may be an anatomical reason related to the shape and size of your vagina. With the latter two, the best course of action is to check with your doctor.

Q. The last few times we have gone to bed I have had problems getting an erection, and then with keeping it for very long. Does this mean I am impotent?

A. Occasional failures can be quite common for most men. They can be brought on by drink, drugs, tiredness, worry, depression, guilt or even fear. If it is only an occasional failure there is little to worry about. Legal and illegal drugs and prescribed medication, can all be responsible, but these can be sorted out by your doctor. Long-term impotence, however, is something that needs to be treated professionally and a variety of treatments are now available.

Q. I'd like to go on the Pill but I have heard that it can have dangerous side-effects. Is this true?

A. If you are overweight, smoke, have a history of heart disease, or come from a family with a history of heart disease, then the Pill may not be right for you. Other side-effects that have been reported are headaches, palpitation, breathing difficulties and chest and leg pains. Most of these can be sorted out by changing the brand of Pill you take. Your doctor or local clinic will give you advice and a thorough examination, including breast examination and a cervical smear, before they prescribe the Pill.

Q. I have never had an orgasm when I make love with my husband. We have tried many different positions and he tries very hard to please me. Does this mean that I never will?

A. Orgasm for women is a complex thing, and something that may have to be learned. The best way is to learn to masturbate yourself to orgasm. Then, involve your partner and teach him what kind of stimulation you like to achieve orgasm. This should allow you to transfer your techniques into your lovemaking sessions and give your partner a good understanding of how best he can assist in helping you achieve your orgasm. During intercourse, you should try using the two 'Fs': friction - in positions which ensure maximum stimulation of a lubricated clitoris, and fantasy – let your mind run free on the imaginings that get you excited during masturbation.

CHAPTER FIVE
KEEPING SEX ALIVE

Help to keep the sparkle in your lovemaking:
intimate times together, sex, fun and fantasy.

REIGNITING THE SPARK

Yes, our sex life had definitely become routine. Then, one evening, we started talking and it got on to sex and how we felt about that. Talking about it turned out to be quite a release – for both of us, and quite a turn on as well. After that we talked more and went back to doing things we hadn't done for ages, Now, if one of us is feeling bored we say so. So far, we've made love in the shower, had oral sex in the car at night, rented some sexy DVDs and played some dressing-up games together, It's fun, it rings the changes, and it sure makes us feel more turned on to each other.

Annie

One of the most common complaints people have about their sex life is that it has become boring, repetitive and lacklustre. It can lose its fizz, and couples may no longer feel the same excitement about one another as they did in the early years of their relationship. Finding a solution to sexual boredom, however, is not always as easy as people may think. For starters, boredom often has nothing to do with what people actually do sexually.

Of course, the same lovemaking routine, which becomes less frequent the longer the couple stay together, can sometimes be frustrating for one or both partners.

Ask yourselves about these three, often interlocking, issues:

- Do we make time for one another?
- Do we communicate?
- Is our sex life exciting?

If the answer to any of these is no, then there is a lot you can do to improve the situation.

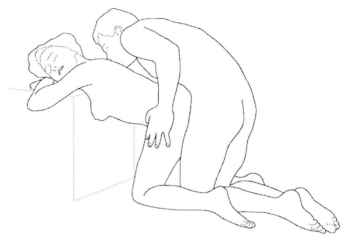

Lack of interest in a relationship may occur if a couple has not spent enough time communicating, or simply because lovemaking bas become routine. Trying new positions, or different locations for lovemaking, can help to revive a flagging sex life. Use your imaginations to think of something new, or try the things you used to enjoy.

I'm sure that we both knew that something was wrong, but we just ignored it. Karen brought more and more work home to do in the evening and I would watch the television, often long after she had gone to bed. It was almost as if we made sure that we never were together enough to talk to each other, let alone have sex. It only started improving when one evening some friends who were coming round had to cancel. We sat down and had the meal together and we were actually forced to talk to each other. And it was a revelation! We make a special effort now to recreate some of the good times we used to have. And I think things will now get even better.

Do we make time for each other?

In the early stages of courtship, finding time for each other is never a problem. Finding each other's company more exciting than one's friends is part of falling in love. Snatching short moments together, seeing each other for lunch even when you are meeting in the evening, are all natural parts of your love life together. Thousands of couples every day call each other just to say "I care about you". But once a relationship becomes permanent, it is all too easy to forget how important these things are – for both of you.

Remember those things that were special to you in the early days, and try to introduce them into your life again. Try hard not to take each other for granted outside the bedroom, and you will not do so inside it either.

Do we communicate?

Communicating about sex is essential to building a good life together. It is often easier before the relationship is signed and sealed. Once we have settled down with someone, we are expected to know how to keep the relationship going and growing. However, many people find it difficult to keep sex and romance alive, especially over many years.

Make the time to talk to one another regularly and at length – and not only about sex but also about everyday life. The experience of marital therapists reveals that, for too many couples, partners really do not understand what the other feels about things as diverse as food, politics, sport or even where they would enjoy going on holiday.

Is our sex life still exciting?

A good relationship can overcome an imperfect sex life. Nonetheless, it is worth asking yourselves the question: "Am I a sexual bore?"

Most couples experiment with different things as they grow closer together, and then settle down to the pattern that suits them best. But preferences change over time: in music, in clothes, even food. So why not in our sex lives? Ask yourselves, "When did we last explore something new sexually?"

SEX AIDS AND TOYS

I suppose our sex life had got a bit boring – and Paul must have thought so too, because one evening he brought a vibrator home with him. I pretended I thought it was a stupid idea, but actually just thinking about it made me feel more turned on than I had for some time. I said I'd try it myself first, and I just started around the inside of my vagina – it was amazing! The sensations were so different to hands and fingers, really exciting. When Paul started using it around my clitoris I was ready to climax so quickly... We made love for ages that night – it was great to start off with the vibrator and then for him to take over with his hands, mouth and penis. We don't use it all the time, but if one of us gets it out, we know it's going to be good...

Diana

Sex aids, or perhaps more accurately sex toys, can add a little fun and variety to your sex life from time to time. Most of the ones you can buy from retail or online shops are safe, and are much better in being designed for the purpose rather than improvising with anything you find around the house. Statistics suggest that around half of all women in the Western world between the ages of 18 and 60 use sex toys and, of those, a remarkable 78% do so within their relationship.

Women who use sex toys tend to experience more frequent and stronger orgasms, have greater sexual confidence and report deeper satisfaction with their partners than women who don't.

The sophistication of the tools human use has been a measure of human progress, and sex is no exception. Curiosity and an instinctive desire to enjoy greater physical pleasure has meant that people have looked for new ways to enhance sexual experience. In ancient times, olive oil was used as a lubricant, condoms were made from goats' bladders and dildos chiseled out of ivory, bone and stone. In the Renaissance, Italians enjoyed the delights of elaborately carved marble *diletti*.

By the Victorian era, sexual indulgence was being suppressed and punished. One flipside, though, was an illness known as hysteria, literally: "womb disease", was cured by sympathetic doctors, who would offer manual relief from its symptoms of rapid heart rate, pelvic heaviness and vaginal lubrication by bringing the patient to orgasm. Then in 1883, a British doctor, Joseph Mortimer Granville, patented the first electromechanical vaginal and clitoral massaging device, a steam-driven monster, and the vibrator was born.

Back in 1999, sex toy retailer Ann Summers was launched on the UK high street and they sold one million vibrators in the first year alone. Twenty years later, luxury brands such as

Coco de Mer, Shiri Zinn and Kiki Montparnasse service the new top end market.

Today the global sex toy industry is valued at over $15 billion, with much of its recent growth due to internet availability, which offers convenient anonymity to both men and women. At the click of a mouse shoppers can venture into a virtual store they may not wish to be seen in real life. It is private and safe at such reputable website shops such as *The Lovers' Guide* one at *www.loversguide.com*.

In modern sex toys, form follows function and new technologies are continually driving innovation. There's the We Vibe which can be used during penetrative sex to stimulate both the man and women. There's the OhMiBod vibrator which uses an iPod playlist to create corresponding beat-driven vibrations. And there's the double-bullet cock ring which activates every time a call or text message is received.

Vibrators

These are probably the most popular sex toys. They are mostly battery-operated, but some of the more expensive models plug into the mains. By and large, it is women who find them the most pleasurable, although some men also find that they create sensual feelings.

Try out a vibrator on yourself before you involve your partner.

A vibrator can be used on any part of the body, so begin by exploring: you will be surprised at the areas of your body that feel good. If the vibrator has a control, try different speeds and discover which body areas are most stimulated.

Explore your genitals.

For a woman, start the vibrator at medium speed and run it along the inside of your thighs and over the whole pubic area. Try stimulating the area between your vagina and anus, as this can be particularly sensitive in many women. Use the vibrator along the inside of your outer lips, up towards the clitoris.

Direct stimulation of the clitoris might be too powerful, or even painful, so experiment until you find the right speed and the exact spot that produces the most pleasurable sensations.

Now try the vibrator inside your vagina, but make sure that you are well lubricated. If you are not, use a little saliva or a proprietary lubricant to help you insert it gently. Experiment with vibrating different parts of your vagina – the entrance, deep against the cervix, or on the front wall to stimulate the G-spot. Find out what you like best. Some women can reach orgasm very quickly and easily this way.

The Rabbit is one of the world's best selling sex toys, known variously as the Jack Rabbit, the Rampant Rabbit and the Jessica Rabbit. A Japanese designer in the eighties combined the range of vibrations available through the main shaft of a regular vibrator with fluttering ears for simultaneous clitoral stimulation. It shot to fame when Charlotte in the TV series *Sex and the City* developed a dependency on hers.

It was one of the first toys I ever tried and the orgasm it delivered matched the best I'd ever had with a lover. I had tears streaming down my face and was genuinely emotional from the experience my Rabbit gave me. The clitoral stimulator, rotating shaft and the swirling bubblegum machine balls in the base combined to make it feel as if I was having the best sex of my life at the same time as a dexterous tongue was working its magic: an experience that's impossible to emulate, I'd say, short of group sex.

Helen

It can be such an intense experience that many women begin only by using the vibrating bunny ears on their clitorises. The shaft and bunny ears tend to be operated with different buttons, so try using each of the available options individually to see which one(s) you like best. Some women like to plunge the Rabbit up to the hilt in one move, while others like to slip it in millimeter by millimeter. Either way, once the Rabbit is a few inches inside you, it's well worth turning on the rotating shaft to stimulate your G-spot. Many Rabbits have shafts that can rotate in both directions so try it each way to see which you prefer and some even find that they ejaculate with such intense stimulation.

Try all the different speed settings, too. Some women like maximum buzz while others like a gentler thrill and it's only by experimenting that you will discover what you most enjoy. One of the advantages of the Rabbit is that it can be controlled with one hand, leaving the other one free to caress erogenous zones such as your nipples, or stroke your clitoris, should you opt for using the Rabbit with the ears on your anus.

Although vibrators can be great fun, they also have an important use for a woman who needs a lot of stimulation before she can have an orgasm. Fingers and the penis can become tired, while a vibrator will carry on steadily for as long as is required to provide the necessary stimulation. By using a vibrator, a woman can help herself achieve her orgasm and then use her own or her lover's fingers, or his penis in similar ways to achieve the same result.

Once you've got used to using a vibrator alone, show your partner what you've discovered. It can help to use it together to arouse the woman before intercourse or to bring her to orgasm. It can work best for couples if the woman first shows the man how and where the vibrator gives her the most pleasure, as the sensations can be quite powerful. You do not need to confine its use to the genitals. Many parts of a woman's body, especially her breasts, are extremely sensitive to this kind of stimulation.

For most men, using a vibrator to stimulate their partner is very exciting. This is especially true if the man feels in control, and can tease his partner to the edge of orgasm and then stop, building up the excitement until he makes love to her himself or to bring her to a climax with the vibrator.

Some women – and their men – fear that they will become addicted to a vibrator, and that intercourse will not then give the same pleasures. The man may even feel he is now redundant. This is rarely the case: a vibrator should be used as a helpful and a fun sex aid – and that is all it should be, not a replacement for a real lover.

Dildos

A dildo is a penis-like object that is designed especially to penetrate the vagina or anus, usually made of latex rubber, and are easy to use if they are well lubricated. The greatest users of dildos are women who like to masturbate with something inside their vagina. But they also can be used during foreplay by either partner.

While the clitoris is stimulated by hand, a dildo can be held still or thrust in and out, either deeply or shallowly according to what creates the most pleasure. It is particularly useful when the woman requires a lot of thrusting to reach a climax, And unlike a penis, it is tireless.

Other stimulators for the vagina are also available. Latex finger covers, for example, which exist in a variety of shapes and sizes, can be used by both men and women. So-called love eggs or Ben-Wah balls are specially designed objects that can be carried around inside the vagina; they come with or without vibrator units.

A word of warning, however. Whilst sex toys designed for the purpose are very safe, do not be tempted to use any penis-shaped object you might find. Never put anything that is breakable into the vagina, nor any spherical object that could easily become trapped when the vaginal muscles contract at orgasm. It could require surgery to remove such an object.

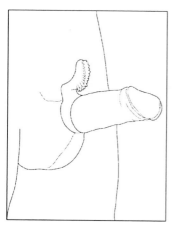

Clitoral stimulators are designed, as the name suggests, to provide pressure and movement on the clitoris during intercourse. They are attached to a ring that is fitted around the base of the man's penis. For some women they can be a great success, but for others they can just be painful or annoying so always be very gentle when you use one for the first time, and consult your partner about how she feels.

Condoms

There is a huge variety of shapes and sizes of textured condoms available. Each can be used on the man's penis, vibrator or dildo, and provide a different sensation to the vagina, although some women feel no effect at all. When used on the penis it is essential to treat them in the same way as standard condoms. They are not just a toy, they are a contraceptive precaution as well. Do not ever re-use one; an unwanted pregnancy would be too high a price to pay for a bit of fun.

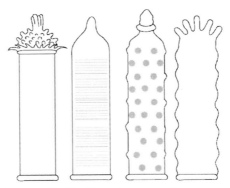

Textured condoms can add a bit of fun to intercourse. For some women they create different sensations in the vagina; for others, however, they have no effect at all.

I've got to admit that we have great fun with those funny-shaped condom things. Jen brought a load home from a hen party and we had a huge trying-on session. By the time I had tried about six, I had such a big erection – Jen wanted to try on more but I couldn't wait any longer and literally leapt on her. It wasn't the fact that they actually enhanced our sensations but all that intimacy was just great.

Oliver

For him

Sex toys that are directly pleasurable to men are finally beginning to develop significantly, particularly over the last decade or so.

For many men, vibrators rarely provide the same amount of pleasure and are unlikely to produce an orgasm. Some, however, do enjoy certain parts of their body stimulated, and some find it pleasurable to have their genitals vibrated. The tip of the vibrator placed gently against the frenum and run around the rim of the penis can create exciting sensations or even an orgasm. There are also special vibrators for anal stimulation including the male G-Spot found on the front wall of his lower bowel.

A major breakthrough came with the creations of special penile sleeves used as masturbation devices, the most notable one being the Fleshlight. It began life in 1998 when a former US police officer, who was looking for a way to deal with a period of enforced abstinence due to his wife's pregnancy, patented a "device for discreet sperm collection". He synthesised a vaginal tunnel – disguised, as its name suggests, as a flash light. Two million dollars of product development brought it to market and the Fleshlight is now the world's number one best-selling sex toy for men.

Penile stimulators are rings that fit over the penis with a small vibrating unit attached which are often also used for masturbation. In a relationship, they have some use for maintaining an erection, and can be pleasurable if the woman uses them to tease her partner by bringing him close to orgasm several times.

Penile rings are specially made to fit around the base of the penis. They will result in the man having a bigger erection, as the blood that would naturally flow out of the penis into the circulatory system becomes trapped, and the penis swells further. This can have advantages for both partners. For the man, the fact that he has a big erection is a turn on in itself; and as most women find that the width of a penis is more important than the length, the woman can experience new and pleasurable sensations. Make sure that the ring is the right size: too small a ring will be painful, and too large a ring will be ineffective. Put it on when the penis is floppy, or it may be impossible to get it on even a semi-erect penis.

After climax, the man should wait until his erection has gone before trying to remove the ring, otherwise in can be painful.

Less than 20 years ago, the idea of a woman using a strap-on dildo to penetrate her male partner anally, would have been shocking. Now such 'back-door' toys – capable of stimulating the male G-spot, or prostate gland - are available at all good sex stores and even on Amazon.

It is completely natural for couples to want to experiment with lovemaking and enhance it in all kinds of ways. Sex toys are just another way of satisfying a natural wish for variety and novelty and, while increasing the excitement, help them stay faithful to their relationship.

LOVE GAMES

The first time, Wendy really took me by surprise! I thought she was having a bath, The next thing I know, she's practically breaking down the bedroom door, and standing there, legs apart, all in black with her little boots, tiny panties, open studded leather waistcoat with nothing on underneath, peaked cap and sunglasses, She told me I had to do everything she said, and then pulled a dildo from the back of her panties. I'm telling you, we had fantastic sex, and now I'm planning a little surprise of my own.

Robbie

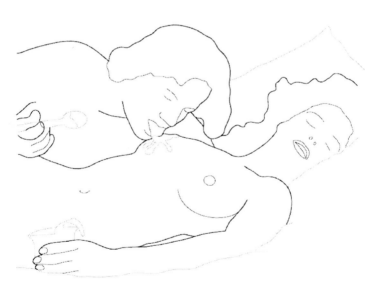

Licking foods such as yoghurt, cream or honey off your lover's body can be highly erotic.

Many couples enjoy adding to their foreplay and arousal by playing games from time to time, just for fun. Most use them as enhancers, to increase their sexual range and to tailor make their sex, so that it encompasses the variety of both their preferences.

Games come in three basic kinds: teasing games, games of skill or chance for sexual favours, or role-playing games. Each couple invents their own rules; the important thing is to ensure that you both know them and agree to abide by them.

Teasing games

The simplest game is for a couple to have a secret code word that means "I want sex". It can be great fun, when you are out in a public place with other people, to build up anticipation by dropping the word into the conversation. An extension of this is to expose parts of your body to your partner so that only he or she can see them.

Another prop for a tease game is a blindfold. Providing that it is not tied on too tightly, it can help you discover new sensations from all your usual lovemaking activities. Removing the sense of sight sharpens the other senses and should heighten your response to touch. Massage, masturbation and oral sex can all feel completely different when you indulge your fantasies.

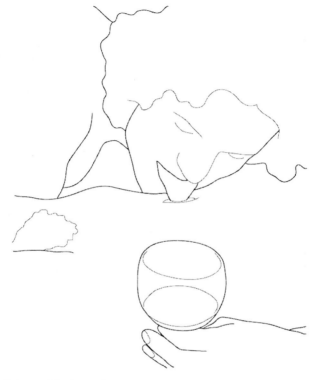

Licking soft foods or different kinds of drinks from your partner's body can be a sensuous experience. The art is to put them on the parts that you know are sensitive to being kissed or licked. Then lick slowly, using your tongue to tease and heighten the pleasurable feelings.

I've always had a thing about soldiers – or any men in uniform, really. I think it's the idea that they're so controlled and untouchable on the outside, but inside... who knows? Nick was in a revue at work, a skit about soldiers, and when he tried on his costume at home, and sort of played the part a bit, it gave me a real thrill. He could see I was excited, so he kept going, and while I tried to turn him on, he made out he wasn't interested at all. In the end, of course, he couldn't hide it and we ended up making love on the kitchen table.

Bianca

Games of chance and skill

All kinds of sexual board games are available from most sex shops, although they are usually rather contrived and expensive. Any board or card game you already have can easily be adapted. All you need to do is to decide on a points system that can be traded for sexual favours. The possibilities for Scrabble or Monopoly are endless, and even computer games can provide new sexual challenges.

Role-playing

These usually involve some form of dressing up, to give the characters you are going to play an appearance of authenticity. They can take many forms you like: doctors and nurses, French maids, generals or nuns. Choose whatever works for both of you. It can be fun to work out the storyline together, and the kind of people the characters are. Doing this is also a good way of communicating your wishes or fantasies, which may be difficult to express in other circumstances. If you want, you might even want to take it further and record the play on video.

It is important to remember that any love game should be fun for both partners, and that for most couples it is only an occasional extra. If they are not pleasurable, then they are not worth playing. And if one of you is shy, it can take some time to get used to the new situation and the often high levels of arousal such games can produce.

Always be guided by your partner's feelings, and begin each new game gently: then you cannot go far wrong.

We were playing Monopoly one evening and I was losing, as usual. Then I landed on one of Henry's properties and I didn't have enough money to pay the rent. Henry said that he would let me off if I took my bra off – so I did. From then on I suppose you can guess what happened. Then we invented a complete payment system which included undressing, oral sex and different positions. It really makes the game much more fun and I certainly don't mind losing any more.

Georgie

FANTASY

We were having a picnic one summer – in a field, on a rug under a tree. When we'd finished eating and we'd drunk some wine we started kissing and cuddling a bit. I could feel Pete's erection in his jeans, when I heard people's voices not far away. I realised this was a situation I'd often fantasised about: making love out in the open, knowing someone might come by and see you any time. I told Pete, and the idea turned him on too, so we got under the rug. It was quick, but really good, and since then thinking about the real thing has been an even better fantasy.

Zara

Nearly everyone has sexual fantasies, and these serve many purposes. We begin fantasising at a very early age and almost everyone has relived the fantasy of their first sexual experience many times in their minds. Fantasies are invaluable aids to masturbation, enriching the experience until it becomes more than merely a mechanical activity of release. They allow us to bring variety to our sex lives that would be impossible to arrange in real life, as it might threaten even the most stable of relationships.

People can sometimes feel ashamed or guilty about the raunchiness of their private sexual feelings, and so tend to keep quiet about them. Yet most such anxieties are unfounded. For a start, it is almost certain that whatever your fantasies are about, they are shared by a lot of other people. And in any case, remember that it remains only a fantasy and does not necessarily affect the way you are in real life – or even the way you want to behave.

Sharing fantasies

A tricky question for most couples is whether they should discuss the subjects of their fantasies. The golden rule is: only share your fantasy if you feel that it will benefit your relationship. While some sexual fantasies can be divulged, others are best kept to yourself. Common sense should tell you what will harm the relationship.

If you do want to share a fantasy with a lover, then choose a time when you are feeling close and loving together, and talk about it. Start off with something simple, and listen for the response. If all goes well, you can safely work up to more complex themes over a period of time. But never tell a partner about a fantasy merely because you want him or her to know you have one.

You may be surprised, however, to find how responsive your partner is, and very often in a good relationship, the fantasies of both partners mesh happily together. But be prepared too for an unexpected response. Respect the fact that your partner may also have fantasies and that they may vary from yours, Women can often have a much richer fantasy life than men; and men are often more shocked at their partner's ideas rather than the other way round.

One way of discovering how your partner will react to your fantasy is to observe his or her response to something that describes it, for example in a magazine, film or video.

Common fantasies

Probably the most common fantasy is that of calling up images of the times when sex seemed perfect. Everyone carries treasured moments from their sexual life, and brings them into play when they make love. This kind of fantasy does much to enrich lovemaking, and can be a powerful trigger to arousal and orgasm.

There are several other fantasies that men and women share.

For instance, dominating and being dominated, which includes bondage and being forced to have sex, is quite common – though this may often involve our current lover or someone familiar. When, for whatever reason someone somehow feels that sex is something they should not initiate, nor even enjoy, it can be a great release to feel that since they cannot be blamed for the act, they can really let themselves go.

Unusual settings for sex also figure high on the list of fantasies. Some women dream of exotic romantic locations such as tropical islands, while some men may prefer to fantasise about daring sex acts in semi-public places like trains or hospitals.

Group sex is also a favourite fantasy for many; the idea of being attended to by two or more other people, or being watched while you and they make love, is enduringly popular.

Common female fantasies (in no particular order)

- Lovemaking with a mystery man/stranger
- Solo sex as partner watches
- Sexual activities with an animal
- Group sex – both with 2 or more women or more men
- Sex in exotic/romantic locations
- Being forced to have sex
- Being tied up for sex
- Sex with another woman
- Dominating a male sex slave
- Sex with a former lover
- Working as a prostitute
- Exhibitionism - as a stripper or being watched having sex
- Voyeurism - watching her partner have sex with someone else/others have sex

Common male fantasies (in no particular order)

- Group sex – with 2 or more women or men or both
- Oral sex – freely or by acting out forcing the woman
- Anal sex with a woman
- Woman using a dildo for anal sex on him
- Sex with another female – neighbour, colleague, partner's sister/best friend/celebrity
- Sex with a man
- Forcing a woman to have sex
- Being dominated/forced to have sex
- Sex with a virgin
- Videoing sex
- Voyeurism - watching a woman masturbate/two women or another couple have sex
- Sex in public places

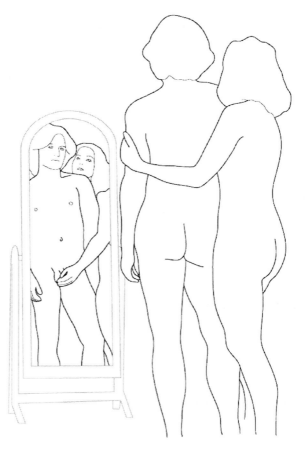

Both men and women may fantasise about having group sex, or sex with more than one person at the same time and watching, and being watched by, other people. A safe and gentle way to act out such a fantasy is to arrange one or two mirrors in the bedroom to create the illusion and without any of the risk that acting out the fantasy in real life could be to your relationship.

My husband reminisced about how the girls wore their skirts so short at school so when I was clearing out and came across my old school tie, I just had to go for it. In the department store I asked the assistant for some of those heavy cotton gym knickers to fit me. The guilt of what I had on my mind must have made me look so suspicious. So I added hastily, "You know, those ones which are really warm and good for skiing". She gave me such a look! After his school kit treat I told him this story about the knickers and he just couldn't stop laughing.

Lily

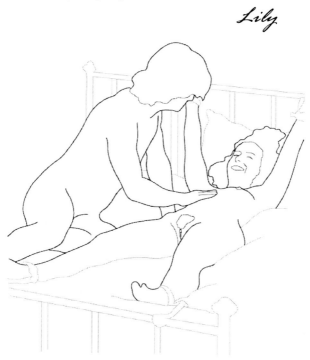

Acting out any form of restraint fantasy should be treated carefully. Never make the bonds too tight and always agree on a word that means "Release me now"– and always stick to it. Tease your partner with a tongue bath or a slow massage with oils.

If you like you can try other erotic touches: feathers, fur, or even your hair. Refrain from intercourse for as long as possible.

KEEPING SEX ALIVE

Acting out our fantasies

Acting out any fantasy that involves tying one another up should be treated carefully. Never put anything around the neck or across the mouth, as this can be extremely dangerous. Agree on the rules, the most important one being the signal to be released. This should always be acted upon immediately.

Use soft materials, such as a tie or silk scarf, for the bonds, and do not tie them tightly – bows are better than knots. When your partner is restrained but comfortable, you can give him or her memorable orgasms by the techniques of slow masturbation or slow oral sex, or massaging with oils, fur, feathers or even your hair – but avoid the genitals for as long as you can. Build up the arousal gradually. The man, for example, can run his penis over the woman's body, or masturbate himself in front of her to increase the excitement.

Next, move to the genitals. The art is to slowly stimulate your partner, either manually or orally, until he or she is at the edge of orgasm – and then to stop. You can do this as many times as you like, but the aim is to make the restraint work for the receiver, and build up to a memorable orgasm.

Dressing-up fantasies are probably the easiest to satisfy, and many love games involving dressing up are ways of acting out fantasies.

Whatever fantasy you decide to act out, make sure that no physical or emotional harm occurs. And be prepared for disappointment: there is no guarantee that in real life your fantasy will live up to your imagination. The dream might even be lost forever.

LOCATIONS

Around the house

On holiday, we went down to the beach one evening and it was completely deserted, so we decided to go for a swim. We just stripped off and ran in naked. Then we made love in the water, me floating on my back with my legs apart and him pulling me backwards and forwards on to him. It was absolutely glorious. At night, under the stars, it was very romantic.

Harriet

Although most couples make love in bed, every home provides a host of interesting locations to add fun and variety to lovemaking. The sitting-room - with plenty of useful props to increase your pleasure - is the most popular venue after the bedroom, though it is probably wise to pull the curtains first.

The floor is a good firm surface in itself, and chairs provide all sorts of possibilities. A sofa can be made excellent use of; try a rear entry position, with the woman leaning on the arm. Her weight is supported so she is comfortable, and she can move backwards and forwards to control the rhythm of thrusting. It is possible to achieve very deep penetration in this way.

It's just great to make love in different places other than the bedroom. I reckon we've made love in every room in the house, and even on the stairs. Somehow it makes things special every now and then.

Isabelle

The kitchen and bathroom

Great sex can be had all around the house. Try it in the kitchen - and, for a really thrilling experience, try it on top of the washing machine on 'high-spin cycle'.

Plenty of romantic and sensuous opportunities here. Bathing together is a pleasure in itself, especially if you take turns to gently soap and wash one another in every place imaginable. A good position to try is for the man to lean back with his weight on his elbows, while his partner sits astride him and also leans back perhaps with her ankles over his shoulders. The feeling of weightlessness provided by the water, the warmth, and the physical closeness, make this an exceptionally exciting position.

Love in the open air

For spicing things up, making love in places other than the bedroom can bring a touch of excitement and naughtiness, which can be highly arousing. And don't forget that making love out of doors need not necessarily involve intercourse.

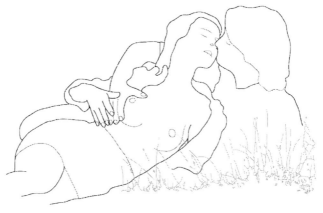

There is no need to confine your lovemaking to the bedroom, or only to evenings and nights. Making love out of doors once in a while, if the time is right and you both want to, can provide wonderful sensual pleasures.

Sex out of doors creates – or rekindles – memories of courtship. In warm weather it can be idyllic for lovemaking. Part of the thrill for many couples lies in the danger that they may be discovered, and the feeling that the whole thing is naughty can have a great aphrodisiac effect.

Satisfying fantasies of exotic locations can be impractical unless you can afford the air fare to a desert island, but outdoor locations can still be exciting. It is not even necessary to go as far as finding a park – especially when making love in public places is illegal (be careful not to fall foul of the law) – so you could settle for a secluded part of your garden.

SPECIAL TIMES TOGETHER

Until we went away for that weekend, I had forgotten that sex wasn't something you just had when you could fit it in. We had all the time in the world and so we could take as much time as we wanted. In fact the first night we didn't have sex at all. We just talked until we fell asleep in each other's arms. The next morning was terrific and we took as much time as we needed. Yes, we're going to do it again soon.

Keith

Every relationship can benefit from setting aside special times just for each other, especially as the years go by; many people can become lazy about the quality and the amount of time they spend together. As a result, their intimate life falls short of what they would like it to be or in some cases fails altogether.

How can we make the time?

If you have a heavy work load and/or if you have young children, it is never easy. The important thing is, to make the effort for yourself, for your partner and for your relationship. Try asking relatives to look after the children from time to time.

A few hours together, alone, will be a wonderful oasis of peace in a hectic life; but occasionally, take it further. Take a long lunch, a day off from work, or go away for a weekend. Make sure that you are both up for it; one partner simply nagging "I need a break" can easily make the other simply feel resentful.

Once you have agreed a time to spend together, it can be fun and exciting for both of you to plan it, and therby increase the anticipation. Remember what it was like when you first fell in love. Send love notes to each other, send flowers or gifts to work with a secret note. Build up the sexual tension through romantic gestures. And when the time comes for you to be together, do not rush into things. Spend time talking, massaging and caressing each other, and generally showing the loving behaviour you used to in the early stages of your relationship. Only you can know whether you want to recapture your earlier times together, or if the time is right to try something new. Be guided by your feelings and those of your partner.

It is important to make a positive effort to create special times.
They give you an opportunity to return to your old intimacies, or perhaps
to discover things for the first time, even after many years together. This is
an investment that will ensure maximum pleasure most of the time. And it
makes other members of the opposite sex seem a very poor second best.

I've been lucky. Mike has always bought me flowers and little presents all the time we've known each other. And then he goes for the big surprise sometimes and comes home with tickets for a long weekend away. I really appreciate all his efforts and I make sure that he knows I do. I'm sure it's helped us get through some of the difficult patches that everyone must have.

Gail

QUESTION TIME

Q. I really enjoy using a vibrator on myself to bring myself to a climax but I am worried that I might become addicted to it and lose interest in having sex any other way. Is it possible?

A. It is extremely unlikely that anyone would ever become addicted to a love toy. Very occasionally, people can develop a fetish about an inanimate object and are unable to enjoy sex unless they use that object during any sex act. But this kind of problem needs professional counselling. For the vast majority of people, really satisfying lovemaking comes from the emotional togetherness of a couple in conjunction with the physical pleasures.

Although vibrators can produce intense physical sensations that a penis cannot always match, the intimacy in a loving relationship should always be more powerful in providing the complete fulfilment that most people seek.

Q. Sometimes when I am making love to my present girlfriend I fantasise about making love to one of my old girlfriends. Does this mean I'm still in love with my ex?

A. Probably not. Men commonly fantasise about making love to other women.

In adolescence, men use fantasies while they masturbate, either from sexy images from magazines, or a series of mental images of a particularly erotic situation. This behaviour is carried over, to a certain extent, into a man's lovemaking.

Imagining back to a "perfect" lovemaking session can help a man maintain his erection for a good deal longer and perhaps even achieve orgasm during a lovemaking session that, for some reason, may not be as exciting as at other times.

Q. We have been together for some time now and our sex life is fine, though I have some fairly wild fantasies that I'd like to act out with my partner. But I just don't know how to tell her about them as I am afraid she might think that I am some kind of pervert.

A. If you think that acting out your fantasies will damage your relationship permanently, then it may be best not to share them. However, it could be that your partner also has fantasies that have parallels with yours. One way to introduce your fantasies is to show each other erotic books, magazines or videos that have similar subject matter and see how your partner reacts to the ideas. If your partner finds them distasteful or offensive it would then be best to keep your fantasies to yourself. But don't be surprised or shocked if she has some out-there ideas of her own, too.

Q. I sometimes like being tied to the bed by my husband when he makes love to me. Does this mean that I'm a masochist?

A. For many women, the desire to be dominated – and equally for many men the desire to dominate and, let's face it, vice versa – during lovemaking is a common occurrence. The fantasy and the reality of being restrained and being forced to have sex is one way of surrendering oneself completely to the other and at a deeper level may be a way of coping with any unconscious guilt feelings about sex that can occur.

Q. Are there any love potions that will make me feel more sexy?

A. So-called love potions, or aphrodisiacs, have been used throughout history. None work, and many have achieved their status such as figs, asparagus or oysters simply because of their resemblance in appearance to, and even smell of, human genitalia. Some which work as internal irritant-stimulants, such as Spanish Fly, are extremely dangerous and can be lethal. Go no further than having romantic dinners to create an eroticism that makes you both feel sexier. In reality the best aphrodisiac is the physical and emotional interaction of a great sex life together.

FURTHER VIEWING AND READING

LOVERS' GUIDE PROGRAMMES

- *The Lovers' Guide* 60min 1991
- *The Lovers' Guide: Making Sex Even Better* 60min 1992
- *The Lovers' Guide: How to Intensify Lovemaking* 90min 1993
  - o Released as: *Better Orgasms For Her* 53min
  - o And: *Better Orgasms For Him* 53min
- *The Essential Lovers' Guide* 77min 1995
- *The Lovers' Guide: Secrets of Sensational Sex* 67min 1999
- *The Lovers' Guide: What Women Really Want* 51min 2002
  - o Includes TV documentary: *The Making of The Lovers' Guide* 48min
- *The Lovers' Guide: Sexual Positions* 55min 2003
  - o Includes special feature: *Interview With The Lovers' Guide Creator* 15min
- *The Lovers' Guide: Sex Play* 56 min 2004
- *The Lovers' Guide: Satisfaction Guaranteed* 57min 2005
- *The Lovers' Guide Interactive* 3 x 55min 2008
- *The Lovers' Guide 3D Igniting Desire* 66mins 2011

Available from www.loversguide.com

BOOKS

Thousands of books have been published about sex and relationships. Many have become bestsellers while others have made an important contribution to the literature on the subject.

Below are listed several titles that we recommend to readers of *The Lovers' Guide* who wish to explore their sexuality and relationships further:

- *Erotic Massage* - Anne Hooper
- *How to Give Her Absolute Pleasure & How to be a Great Lover* - Lou Paget
- *Improving Your Relationship For Dummies* - Paula Hall
- *Multi-Orgasmic Couple* - Mantak Chia
- *My Secret Garden, Women on Top & Men in Love* - Nancy Friday
- *O: The Intimate History of the Orgasm* - Jonathan Margolis
- *Sex in Loving Relationships* - Sarah Livinoff
- *Sexual Body Talk* - Susan Quilliam
- *She Comes First* - Ian Kerner
- *Super Hot Sex & Hot Relationships* - Tracey Cox
- *The Art of Sensual Loving, The Loving Touch & The Joy of Sexual Fantasy* - Andrew Stanway
- *The Complete Idiot's Guide to a Healthy Relationship & To Dating* - Judy Kuriansky
- *The G Spot* - Alex Kahn Ladas, Beverly Whipple and John D Perry
- *The Guide to Getting It On* - Paul Joannides
- *The Joy of Sex* - Alex Comfort
- *The Lovers' Guide Encyclopaedia* - Doreen E. Massey

- *The Science of Orgasm* - Barry R. Komisaruk, Carlos Beyer-Flores and Beverly Whipple
- *The Sex Book* - Suzi Godson
- *The Story of V* - Catherine Blackledge
- *The Ultimate Guide to Fellatio & The Ultimate Guide to Cunnilingus* - Violet Blue
- *The Whole Lesbian Sex Book* - Felice Newman
- *Ultimate Gay Sex* - Michael Thomas Ford

ABOUT

The Editor

Robert Page MA first created *The Lovers' Guide* on video in 1991 and has supervised its growth into one of the world's most authoritative sex education series. It has been released as over a dozen DVDs, three books, including an Encyclopedia, several TV documentaries and one of the biggest sex education websites on the internet: *www.loversguide.com*. As a producer and CEO of the Lifetime Group, he has also produced many other TV series and films, including the award-winning *Floyd On...* for the BBC and Dr Desmond Morris' *The Animal Contract*. He has written and broadcast widely and is a member of various professional organisations for sexual counselling and research, including AASECT, WAS, SSSS and BASE. He currently lives in New York with his wife and has two sons.

The Consultant

Dr Andrew Stanway MB, MRCP, is a qualified psychosexual and marital physician. He presented the first four of *The Lovers' Guide* video series and has written over 30 books on sex, medicine and health. He has broadcast widely on sexual and marital matters. He lives in Ireland with his wife and has three daughters.

Lightning Source UK Ltd.
Milton Keynes UK
UKOW052159091112

201970UK00003B/1/P